A Song for Olaf

Mnemosyne Books

Praise for *A Song for Olaf*

Jennifer Boulanger's *A Song for Olaf* is a passionate and personal account of the author's brother's illness and untimely death from AIDS. The story is beautifully and movingly told, bringing tears to my eyes several times. Gay men who have a special bond with a sister will recognize themselves and their siblings in these pages; I know I did. *A Song for Olaf* emotionally evokes the uniqueness of a powerful sibling bond in a time of unimaginable pain and loss. It underscores how the pandemic's toll far exceeds the number of those who have died or are living with HIV today, but encompasses the enormous price paid by those who love us.

—Sean Strub
Activist & Editor of *POZ* magazine
Body Counts: A Memoir of Activism, Sex, and Survival

A Song for Olaf, Jennifer Boulanger's quietly stunning memoir of losing her brother to HIV-AIDS at the dawn of that pandemic, is infinitely more than a vivid portrait of her own struggle with grief. She brings Olaf to such vibrant life for us, in all his youthful promise, that we, too, mourn the author's loss. And with equal passion and prescience at this crucial moment when we are still in the shadow of COVID and awaiting whatever its next iteration will be---Boulanger invites us to ask these urgent questions: What do we as individuals and as a society become, if we surrender to fear, isolate and stigmatize those who are ill, and turn away from our shared human suffering?

In this beautifully-observed life of one man and brother, Jennifer Boulanger holds up a mirror to countless other lives. Even, perhaps, our own.

—Laurie Gunst
Born fi' Dead: A Journey through the Jamaican Posse Underworld
Off White: A Memoir

A Song for Olaf

*A Memoir of Sibling Love at the Dawn
of the HIV-AIDS Pandemic*

By

Jennifer Boulanger

Mnemosyne Books

Published By

MNEMOSYNE BOOKS
An Imprint of

SAINT JULIAN PRESS, Inc.
2053 Cortlandt, Suite 200
Houston, Texas 77008

www.saintjulianpress.com

Print ISBN: 978-1-955194-41-9
eBook ISBN: 978-1-955194-42-6

Library of Congress Control Number: 2025932301

Cover Design: Laura Smyth

This book is dedicated to Olaf's beloved Goddaughter, Sara, who lives by the notion that love is love. And to all the precious souls who have encountered prejudice because of who they love.

All of the events recounted in this book are true.
Out of respect for privacy, I have changed some characters'
names.

A Song for Olaf

Chapter One
1993

I don't know what will happen to me without you. Only you. Only you love me. Out of everyone in the world.

—Tony Kushner, *Angels in America: Part One—Millennium Approaches: A Gay Fantasia on National Themes*

He was Olaf. I was Holine.

I don't really remember where the names came from anymore, but once uttered, they stuck. My brother and I made them up when he was small and I was smaller.

But now we were grown, and he had shrunk back small again, his frail body lost in the folds of an over-washed, white hospital gown. The colorless garment emphasized his already sallow complexion, white verging on gray.

"Not again," Olaf said, his large liquid green eyes filled with weariness. Even his rebellious, free-flowing hair, which he was fond of sweeping back from his forehead, drooped forward, as if tired. Then it happened. He turned to his favorite nurse, Charlotte, whose steady hands had a firm grip on his wheelchair, and I saw something both familiar and surprising in his glance: a telltale glint of humor, a hint of playfulness.

"Are these the only color these come in?" he said, a ghost of a smile tracing across his face. "A paisley print, maybe? These do nothing for my complexion." There was the Olaf I knew

1

bubbling up to the surface, ever the performer, always playing to an audience.

"We'll see what we can do next time," Charlotte laughed. "Now, come on—mask up."

Just moments before, Charlotte had pushed a button prompting the heavy steel doors of the health sciences transfusion center to creak slowly open. A gust of air laden with the stale stench of antiseptic hit us square in the face. Just beyond the door, a stern-looking nurse stopped us, a handful of paper masks dangling from her latex-gloved hands.

Charlotte took the masks and put one on, demonstrating the proper technique for Mom, Olaf and me, who dutifully hooked the elastic bands around our ears and tightened them. The dusty metallic smell rising off the masks penetrated our nostrils, making it hard to breathe. Mom adjusted her mask and pulled at each of the curls that framed her face, ensuring their curve in the right direction. An old-school, dignified woman, she believed in dressing properly for every occasion. And in keeping her emotions in check. Her makeup was meticulously applied, but her painted perfection—now mostly tucked beneath her mask—only emphasized the lost, haunted look in her eyes. I felt her instinctively recoil as we entered the ward.

We slowly made our way into the transfusion center, with its rows of identical narrow beds. The occupants lay, resigned and silent, decaying in succession. Each was alone. Months of illness had left them unconcerned with modesty, so most of the curtains hung open. One after another, ashen-faced men with skeletal bodies reclined, their bony knees pointing upward sharply under their blankets like stakes under a tent. Each had an IV pole and a blood pack, wires and hoses attached to the backs of hands and wrists.

"There's a free bed down this way," Charlotte said, as she briskly pushed the wheelchair to a corner spot. She gently supported Olaf, one arm under this elbow, the other at his waist, as he transferred to the bed. She settled him in, went in search of fresh warm blankets and the transfusion bag, and reappeared in moments.

"Here you go. Now, this is the first one; you'll need two today," Charlotte said as she found the veins under his bruised skin. Olaf winced, his discomfort visible in his downcast eyes. "Not to worry, now. Hour and a half, two hours tops," Charlotte encouraged, then gave him a motherly hug and vanished. Mom gently tucked the warm blankets under Olaf's bony legs.

I found a couple of chairs, and placed one for Mom on one side of the bed, mine on the other. Heaving my heavy book bag onto the floor beside me, I rubbed my aching shoulder.

Pretending we hadn't just passed one dying man after another, with forced cheer Mom said, "Here she goes again, dragging her work everywhere!"

"Ah . . . that's my Holine, always papers to grade," Olaf mumbled through the mask, a tinge of regret in his tone, and it occurred to me how much he missed teaching.

"Yes. Papers! Always papers," I said. "But I don't have to grade them now."

"We're just sitting around anyway, whiling away the lonely hours!" he laughed. "You may as well get some work done. Besides, you can read me the fun parts." Olaf pushed the wheeled hospital tray in my direction to serve as a desk. It was my turn to supply the entertainment, to lighten the mood.

"OK. Let me see," I said, pulling the blue folder overflowing with ESL essays from the bag. I read through three or four, circling words and scribbling corrections while Mom and Olaf stared at the soaps on TV.

"Here's one," I said. I read, "'Because my sister's wedding was happy day, everyone mad was happy again. We all cheered when the groom lifted her veal to kiss her.'"

Olaf laughed, "Veal! That's great."

I read on: "'Even my father decided to borrow the hatchet.'"

Olaf chuckled. "Those pesky idioms! Gets 'em every time."

I leafed through my papers, stopping to skim one that looked promising. "Here's another one: "'Two brothers came with him from Japan,'" I read. "'One was short. One was much higher than the other.'"

"Aw!" Olaf said. "How do you stand it? They are so cute."

"And smart, too," I said. "Their writing is so simple and so beautiful." I found one essay I especially liked. "Listen to this: 'The countryside of my home is green with the garden of my father. He plants with love, so his vegetables grow.'"

"So sweet," Olaf said. I skimmed some more pages.

"There's another one here, if I can find it, where Trin writes about leaving Cambodia." I leafed through the pile again, looking for Trin's distinctive, perfectly-formed script, letters rounded like pansy blossoms. "Yup, this one. Here it is: 'We left Cambodia, the green hills fading away behind us as our boat sailed. I held my children close, the baby on my lap. I looked back one more time. I would never see my brother now. Never again.'"

The words were out of my mouth before I could take them back. I had forgotten the ending of my student's paper, the words that voiced my own fear. When I looked up from the page, Charlotte had returned with a second transfusion bag. Gauging our expressions, she quietly detached the first and hooked the second on the IV pole, then disposed of the first in the red bin, the one marked in bold print: HAZARDOUS WASTE.

I dropped my pen, pushed the mobile table scattered with papers aside, and slid downward from the chair to Olaf's bed, falling in beside him. I wanted to linger there, holding him, remembering all of our moments, who we were to each other, our shared story. And the golden, shimmering gift of unconditional love that Olaf had bestowed on me, his little sister, sidekick and best friend. A future without him was unimaginable. My head burrowed into his frail shoulder, I let the current of memory pull me along, backward, into the past, to the first time I had to let him go.

Chapter Two
1969

A police raid in the Stonewall Inn, a tavern frequented by homosexuals at 53 Christopher St., just east of Sheridan Square in Greenwich Village, triggered a near riot early today. As persons seized in the raid were driven away by police, hundreds of passers-by shouting 'Gay Power' and 'We Want Freedom' laid siege to the tavern with an improvised battering ram, garbage cans, bottles and beer cans in a protest demonstration.

—Village Raid Stirs Melee, *New York Post*

The trees rustled, exposing random red leaves, flashing like hazard lights. The telltale signs were everywhere: the cooler evenings; the fields of ragweed and my itching, watering eyes. Summer would soon be a memory. But one thing was different from every other summer, arching toward autumn: my brother Olaf was leaving for college in just days.

It felt like our family was trying to snatch up the last waning days of togetherness when, one afternoon, Mom and Dad told Olaf and me they were planning to take us on an end-of-summer trip to Saratoga Springs. Right from the start, the whole idea seemed like a false promise, as if they hoped capturing family moments on Polaroids would somehow freeze us forever in August 1969. As I opened the suitcase to pack, I was all too aware that in just a few days we would empty this same suitcase of shorts and flip-flops only to refill it with Olaf's life—his books, his records, his sheet music, his modest wardrobe.

The morning of our departure, when I, still in my nightgown and slippers, wandered out of my bedroom, Olaf burst from the bathroom, his green eyes bright with anticipation under the swoop of thick chestnut hair that swept across his forehead. He was already dressed in his fraying bell-bottom jeans and college orientation t-shirt, which hung off his skinny frame. His flip-flops, worn to postcard thin on one side, clicked in rhythm as he danced his way down the hall.

"C'mon, Holine!" Olaf shouted. "Time's a wasting." He grabbed a backpack from his room and sang his way down the stairs.

A half hour later, we headed east in the morning fog, speeding into the day on the New York State Thruway from Utica. The mist lifted, and the sky ripened into a perfect late summer day. By the time we reached the stretch between Herkimer and Little Falls, the traffic had begun to pick up. Dad slowed down, letting cars pass.

"We're not in any hurry," he said, and contentedly drove along, hovering just under the speed limit. But as the minutes turned into an hour, we inched toward Amsterdam, slowing to a crawl till we were sandwiched between a battered Beetle and a chartered bus. I turned to look out the rear windshield to discover a snaking line of cars behind us, one after another, farther than I could see.

"What in hell is going on with all these cars?" Dad said.

"Do you think there's an accident?" Mom asked and strained in her seat to get a better view.

We peered out the windows at the procession of older Volkswagen vans and Audi clunkers with tents strapped on top, flat-bed trucks stuffed with women in peasant blouses and ankle-length gauze skirts, bearded men with patched jeans, their sandaled feet swinging off the side.

"Dad! Woodstock!" Olaf said. "It's Woodstock! Come on, Dad! Just . . . follow 'em! You keep going to Albany, then—you know—just a quick turn south on 87," he added, matter-of-factly, like it was the most logical suggestion ever.

"Yeah, right," Dad laughed.

"Seriously, Dad!" Olaf teased. "Why not?"

"Sure," Dad said, dripping sarcasm. "I'm going to take your mother to Woodstock." He rolled his eyes toward Mom, who giggled at the thought. It *was* pretty funny to imagine Dad, with his growing-out crew cut, in his green golf shirt with the little Izod alligator logo and Mom, in her flowered pants and matching bag, mingling with face-painted, tie-dyed hippies, a haze of weed smoke swirling overhead.

Olaf and I exchanged a look—*Oh, to be so close and to miss it*—the celebration, the nature, the *music*, all steeped in the super cool peace-and-love vibe. When Dad finally reached the exit to Amsterdam, he breathed a sigh of relief, and we picked up speed again, headed northeast. Olaf, beside me in the back seat, waved his arms madly toward the right, trying to will the car to magically turn in the direction of Yasgur's farm where Crosby, Stills, Nash and Young were probably at that moment stepping off helicopters onto the Woodstock stage.

"You know, kids, we *are* going to a concert." Mom said. "At the new Performing Art Center. You can sit outside and hear the music right from the lawn," Mom said, as if an outdoor concert was some kind of miracle. I didn't have the heart to tell her that going to SPAC felt like the worst consolation prize ever—like those losers on *Let's Make a Deal* who chose the wrong door and get a broken-down jalopy instead of the Corvette.

That weekend we did all the stuff you're supposed to do on vacation: we ate at open-air restaurants, spread our blanket on the lawn in view of the concert stage and bet on long-shots at the racetrack. But we were just marking time, every hour that ticked by adding more and more weight to our hearts. We were running out of days together, Olaf and I. By the end of the trip, even pretending to have fun was difficult. A pall settled over us, as tangible as the pollen sifting through trees, blanketing the cars in a film of green.

"Want a Lifesaver?" he offered wanly, across the back seat. "Butter rum." He waved the pack enticingly.

"Sure," I said, pretending a hoop of colorful candy would lessen my anxiety about the coming change. But I could not escape the reality that my brother Olaf was leaving. A few steps ahead of me in life, he'd always been on his way somewhere else, away from me, where I could not go. When I was a toddler, he was already in grade school. When I was in middle school, he was in high school. Now I was entering high school and he was off to college. An ache lodged in my chest and I wondered: *Who would I talk to now?*

The day after we returned home, I hung around Olaf's room as he lined up hundreds of records in box after box. Next to the boxes, a large, locking trunk was filled with new tan and navy corduroys and mounds of paperbacks. In the corner of the room, Mom ironed plaid shirts, then folded and packed them in ordered stacks in a suitcase. She floated back and forth from the iron to the suitcase, her pink flowered housedress perfectly matching her candy pink lips. From the neck up, you'd have thought she was ready for a night on the town—her flawless makeup accentuated her symmetrical, delicate features, her black hair so shiny it shone almost blue, not a strand of her bubble-cut out-of-place.

"Mom, enough already!" Olaf said, rubbing Mom's shoulder gently. "I don't need all these shirts. Really. What I have packed is plenty." Mom looked into his grateful eyes, He leaned into Mom lovingly and wrapped an arm around her. Then, she stood the iron up on its end. As it hissed a final blast of steam, she propped both palms firmly against the ironing board as if she might suddenly collapse without support.

"Mom, it's OK!" Olaf said, coaxing her toward the bed. "Sit down a minute. Here, sit."

Mom sat and pulled a tissue from the sleeve of her housedress. I sat too, sliding down the wall to the carpeted floor. I squeezed my eyes shut against my rising tears. Then Mom dabbed at her mascara-runny eyes, and whispered, "I'm sorry. It's just . . . the shirts."

"The shirts?" he asked, sitting down beside her. "What about the shirts, Ma?'

"It's just . . . I'm so used to taking care of you."

"Hey! What do you mean? You're not going to stop taking care of me, are you?" Olaf asked in a gentle tone. "You're not getting off that easy," he teased. "I'm bringing my laundry home every week! Don't forget, Ma; I'll be home every Saturday to work at the radio station. And I expect all my shirts to be clean and pressed before I drive back on Sunday!" Olaf gave her a squeeze, and she laughed a little, though her tears continued to flow.

"I know, I know," she said, wiping her eyes. "It's silly. I'll see you in a week. It's just . ." she faltered.

"You'll see. You'll get sick of me, I'll be home so often," Olaf said, and, looking at me, added, "Tell her, Holine! In a few days, you'll all be saying, 'Are you home *again*?'" But I could only manage a nod. Olaf looked from me to Mom, and, gazing into her worried eyes, he studied her carefully for some moments, then flashed his sweetest look and an encouraging smile.

"Just let me finish this one last shirt," she said, wiping her eyes. She stood and ironed the last sleeve, then folded the shirt neatly and placed it on top of the pile in the suitcase. After that, Mom wandered in and out with plastic bags full of sheets, pillows, towels. She asked random questions about meal passes and hotpots and parking permits. Out of excuses, she looked from side-to-side, her hands fluttering, needing to keep busy. Finally, she walked out and clip-clopped down the stairs to find something to cook or clean.

I didn't know what to do with myself either. I paced nervously, then finally turned to go hide out in my room.

"Wait a sec, Holine," Olaf said. He fumbled through the pile of paperbacks in the open trunk and pulled out a slim volume. "Here—you can have this. You're gonna love it." It was his Folger's edition of *A Midsummer Night's Dream*, the kind with the explanations on every other page. I thanked him, hugged it to my chest, and walked out. I put the book on the nightstand next to my bed, then turned my face into the pillows.

On any given evening, I would usually find Dad in the den, cozy in his Barcalounger and riveted to the TV, and—depending on the time of year—tucked beneath a Grandma-crocheted lap blanket. His routine was another kind of blanket altogether: the least disruption to his habitual existence sent him reeling. After dinner each day, Dad pushed away from the table and exclaimed, "Time to watch the war on TV" and off he went, newspaper in hand, to sit before the Grand Poobah of TV News, Walter Cronkite. As he settled into his easy chair, in one fluid motion, he pushed up the square-rimmed, dark glasses that had slipped down his nose, then scowled in concentration at the screen as Cronkite enumerated the day's body count. Moments later, a field reporter shouted over the chop-and-swish of helicopters, a tangled jungle his backdrop. Dad stared intensely at the scene that unfolded, his face a mask of alarm.

But when I wandered into the den the night before Olaf left for college, I was surprised to find Dad not watching TV but sitting before the record player. His face overcome with emotion, his eyes brimming, he sat, church-pew still, enraptured as a voice radiant with passion and melancholy rose and fell over the swell of strings, flooding the room.

"Oh. Dad?" I questioned, sensing as soon as I'd spoken that perhaps I should not have. He startled, momentarily shaken from the spell the music had cast. "I'm sorry . . . " I faltered. "Puccini . . . right?"

Dad had spread the creased and yellowed libretto in front of him, just as Olaf and I had done as children, Olaf lying beside me on the floor, pointing out the English translation so I could keep up. Dad silently brushed a tear away with his sleeve.

"Here . . . sit," he said, and gave a pat to the chair as an invitation, sliding over so we could listen together. I tucked myself in beside him, nuzzled against the crispness of his pressed shirt, a trace of his aftershave rooted in the threads. He pointed to the text, helping me to follow the story, just as Olaf had always done. The voice rose above the plaintive strains of a single clarinet, the message of longing and loss expanding forward and upward.

"Cavaradossi . . . the painter . . . remember?"

I nodded. "He's going to be killed, right?"

"Yes," he said, wistfully. "'Disperato!' he says, over and over. It always gets to me."

The piece ended. Dad and I sat quietly a moment, gathering ourselves, restored somehow in the knowledge that Tosca's grand tragedy overshadowed our own: Olaf leaving home. Dad took a deep breath, then folded the libretto and, carefully lifting the record from the turntable, returned both to the sleeve. He inserted them in the cardboard case, black lettering above a photo of Renata Telbaldi on a bright pink background. Suddenly, he turned to me, a sly smile crossing his face.

"Can you keep a secret?" he whispered.

"'Course!" I cried a little too loudly, then, lowering my voice, continued, "You know me: mum's the word." I made a motion as if zipping my lips closed.

Dad turned to his secretary desk and pulled the hinged door down. He peeked my way, pressed his index finger over his mouth as if to say, "Don't tell anyone," and opened the hidden compartment—a rectangular wooden box that slid sideways out of a slot inside the desk. Something within it clacked against the wood as he walked toward me. He turned over the box, delivering to my hand what was hidden inside. It was a single metal key, triangles—or maybe they were mountain peaks?— cut into the end one would turn.

"A key?" I asked. "What's it for?"

"The Beetle!" he whispered. "For your brother."

"What?" I cried. "You're giving him the Volkswagen?"

"'Course." He said it matter-of-factly, but his face was filled with pride. "He's a big college boy now, right?"

"Oh, Dad! He's . . . he's gonna be so surprised!"

"'Till tomorrow: our secret." Dad winked at me.

The next morning by the time I got up, Olaf was at his usual place at the kitchen bar, eating his Lucky Charms and studying the cereal box intently. On the back was a maze with a little leprechaun at the "start," and, between bites, Olaf traced his finger across the possible routes that would lead him to the end of the rainbow. Outside, Dad was already packing the car. I couldn't blame him for wanting to get us out of there. The feeling of loss hung like a line of clouds just over our heads, all of us ducking under it. Dad, Olaf and I avoided eye contact with Mom, who was already hiding behind her sunglasses. In only a half hour we'd be at Utica College, chosen by Olaf so he could keep his job reading news and playing the elevator music favored by our local radio station. Although the campus was closer to our house than the nearest K-Mart, distance wasn't the issue. It was the leaving, our never living together again.

We arrived on campus in mid-morning, me in the Volkswagen with Olaf. Mom and Dad followed in Dad's car, which tailed us down a winding cracked road, white and institutional like the walkways. The campus, a collection of 60's era rectangular buildings--some already missing plaster here, streaking rust there--was compact, only about four or five city blocks long, so we found Olaf's dorm easily.

"This is it, guys! North Hall," Olaf said as Mom and Dad got out and looked around. "See?—over there? That's Strebel Student Center, and next to it, to the right—that's the library." Olaf pointed at the buildings like he had lived there forever, and I was impressed with how much he knew after a one-day orientation. But he talked faster than usual, stiff and jittery.

"Student union?" Dad asked, as he opened the trunk and began unloading suitcases and boxes. "The one with the pub in the basement?"

"Yes," Olaf answered, then exclaimed "Fun times!" but his face twitched as he grabbed a box from the trunk.

"Let's hope you spend more time in that library you pointed out," Dad said, winking at Mom and me.

Olaf stood motionless a moment, staring up at the four-story building that would become his new home. His eyes fluttered. Then he squared his shoulders and looked me in the eye.

"C'mon, Holine," he said. "Let's get this party started." But he looked at me too closely, and noticed me blinking back tears. "It's OK, Holine," he said.

Mom, Dad and I followed Olaf up the stairs to room 208, each side a mirror image of the other: a particle board desk, a narrow, eight-drawer dresser, and a bed with a thin twin mattress pushed against the window. Mom got right to work, unpacking and hanging clothes, making up the bed with new sheets and a comforter that still smelled of plastic, like the store. While she worked, Dad and I trudged up and down the stairs carrying boxes and stereo speakers and crates of shoes and record albums. In his room, Olaf messed with the wires, hooking up the stereo.

As I climbed up the last time, I heard the Joni Mitchell song I knew so well, the familiar lyrics, "Don't give yourself away . . ." warning me to tuck my feelings inside. But in that moment, I wasn't in Utica anymore. I was home, sprawled across a lawn chair on the roof, my hand dangling over the side, fingers drumming against the scratchy shingles. That roof, our hiding place, where Olaf and I had first listened to this song together, speakers propped in the open window. I couldn't hold it in; I began to cry. And then Mom started crying for real, making those little choking sounds she always made when she was trying to stop.

Olaf wrapped one arm around her and the other around me.

"Girls," he said, "I'll see you Saturday—six days from now. Come on, now . . ." But his eyes were sad.

We walked down to the car together, Olaf walking Mom to the Beetle, expecting she would drive it home. "Now, honey," Mom sobbed, "if there's anything you need . . . "

"I know, Ma. It's OK. I'll be fine," he interrupted. But his dark eyes fell, in that way that always broke me in half. Dad came up behind them, and, without saying a word, pressed the VW key into Olaf's palm.

"What's this?" Olaf asked.

"The key," Dad said.

"But, wha . . . "

"To your car," Dad said.

"*My* car?" Olaf asked.

"Yes. *Your* car now."

"Mine?" Olaf cried. "Oh…my God, Dad! You didn't have to…"

"We want you to have it. Your mother and I. So you can get to your job and…you know, come home whenever you want to," Dad said.

"Thanks, Dad, you know…for everything," he said as he turned to Dad. He reached out his hand as if to shake Dad's, and Dad started towards him, his hand extended, then came closer and hugged him tightly instead. I hugged him from behind, so he couldn't see my face, then slipped into the back seat.

I couldn't help looking back at Olaf as we drove away, his slight frame fading in the distance. Already small, he became smaller still. Then we turned a corner, and behind me there was only road.

It seemed as if mere minutes had passed, and I was headed down the hallway of Rome Free Academy, leaving my first day of high school.

The walk home was brutal—not that it was long. Although it was September, it was mid-July hot as I juggled the geometry, world history and physics books and several three-ring binders, shifting them from my left arm to my right every half-block or so. The route was familiar, straight down Linden Street, and directly by our old elementary school.

Just before the turn toward home, I passed the row of apartments near the corner of Linden and Franklyn, the corner that had been a marker for me my whole life. It was the spot I was absolutely forbidden to pass on my new two-wheel bike, the spot where we'd stop, turn, and head toward home again, Olaf holding the back of my seat and giving me a running start to the *click-click-click* of the Mantle card against the spokes. Once, Mom and Dad allowed me to go as far as the apartments to sell Girl Scout cookies, but only if Olaf came along, watching warily from the sidewalk as I wrote my neighbors' names and their orders of Thin Mints and Tag-a-longs on the official order form. Olaf always had to do the math for me in the end, letting the customers know how much they owed.

The Linden corner was also the site of the great snowball ambush of 1960. It was the first time Mom let me walk home from school with a first-grade classmate, Lorraine, instead of Olaf. We had almost made it home, slipping and stumbling through skinny paths between mountains of January snow. When I looked back, I could see Olaf following close behind, keeping me in his sights.

Suddenly, almost at the turn—*whizz-pop*! A snowball hit me, square in the back of my puffy snowsuit. Lorraine got hit next—*whack*!—on her right sleeve. We jumped sideways, almost tumbling into a snowbank, then turned to see them: Bobby Slipnik, his friends Richard and Todd and some older kids we didn't know. They peeked out from behind their hiding place, a snowplow mountain of white across the street. Next to it, they had built towers of snowballs, a pile for each of them so they could fire them at us—*pow, pow, pow, pow, pow*—fast as the gun at the midway.

"Look out!" I heard Olaf yell from somewhere behind us. But before Lorraine and I could stand up straight, we were hit again and again, boys shooting two and three snowballs at a time, this time not at our backs. They got me in the shoulder, the tummy, and then . . . smack, right over my left eye, the icy crust around the snowball piercing the fleshy skin under my eyebrow.

"My eye!" I screamed, and touched my mitten to the spot where the wound stung and tingled. When I saw a dot of blood on the threads, I really started wailing.

Out of nowhere, Olaf's hat bobbed into view. "You hurt my sister!" Olaf screamed as he rushed into the middle of the action.

He went straight for the gang of boys, directly into the line of snow-bullets, picking up snow as he went and trying to form it, but throwing it too soon. Loose little snow mounds barely made it past his boots, and he was hit—*pop-pop-pop-pop-pop*—by so many snowballs, he covered his head with his arms, then turned away so they hit his back instead.

"Sissy!" Bobby yelled after him.

"Yeah, you sissy!" echoed another. "What are *you* gonna do?"

"Sissy! Sissy!!" a chorus of boys joined in.

Pop-pop-pop-pop-pop. Snowballs pummeled him till he couldn't do anything but turn and run, grabbling my hand as we took off away from the kids, slipping and sliding our way toward home.

When we were far enough away, I looked at Olaf through my tears. That face.

And that word. That word that hurt us more than the snow. That word that could not be taken back, said right out loud, that all the kids heard. As he walked me the rest of the way home, I hardly felt the icy slash over my eye. There was a new hurt. We didn't talk the rest of the way, the leftover taste of salt in our mouths.

Finally back home from my first day of high school, I unlocked the back door, the only sound the thump of my books as I dropped them onto the kitchen counter. I had never come home from school to an empty house before. Back when Olaf was home, I'd hear music half a block from the house: blaring organ chords from Olaf's Hammond or harmonies blasting from massive speakers. "Carry on! Love is coming." The silence was unnerving.

I knew I shouldn't do it, but sometimes when you're sad, you just want to be sadder. I went into his room. It was absolutely sterile, as if no one ever lived in it all. No clothes in piles on the floor, no stereo and stacks of records, no books, except a 1962 copy of *Huckleberry Finn* and a Communion prayer book on the nightstand.

Only two other signs of him remained. The bureau's bottom drawer sagged on one side in a lopsided frown, a casualty of the treasures heaped inside it. A few years earlier, Dad tried to fix it. He'd attempted to epoxy the chunk that had broken off the bottom of the drawer, swearing in Italian when it wouldn't hold and then finally chucking the piece across the room in disgust. The stubborn drawer would not become the shiny, good-as-new restoration that he envisioned, no matter how many times he told it to "Go the hell to Naples."

Left behind too were Olaf's old, down-filled pillows. After one too many pillow fights and countless, twitchy, dream-filled nights, they'd shed so many of their feathers, they looked like punctured packing bubbles, flat on the side of the tear. Deep within them, a hint of his scent remained—a damp forehead, muted shampoo, a tinge of his breath from deep, drooling sleep. Mom had slipped freshly laundered pillowcases over the pillows now, but she couldn't cover his essence, stubbornly embedded deep in the feathers. No one was home, so who would it hurt? I pulled the pillows from under the spread and buried my face in them.

Chapter Three
1969

A teenager in St. Louis, Missouri dies after a bout of an inexplicable infection. Only a decade and a half later, his illness is diagnosed as AIDS.

—James Kinsella, *Covering the Plague: AIDS and the American Media*

It started with some serious arm-twisting from Olaf—multiple phone calls with lots of "C'mon, Ma! I'll be her absolute *shadow!* Honest! I won't let her out of my sight!"—while Dad listened in on the extension and eyed me closely, worried I was too young . . . or that I didn't look young enough. Finally, Mom and Dad gave in, bequeathing to us their permission for me to visit Olaf at college. The caveat: a mile-long list of dos-and-don'ts, including such gems as:

> *No parties.*
> *Call us as soon as you get there.*
> *Stick to your brother like glue.*
> *Make sure you eat. And not just the cookies I packed.*
> *Call us before you go to bed.*
> *Don't dare get in a car with anyone but your brother.*
> *Call us when you're ready to leave for home.*
> *No parties. None.*

Of course, the first thing we did was find a party in the dorm's study lounge.

Two big honking speakers blared *Gimme Shelter* from a couple of study carrels on one side of the room; a keg sat in a tub of ice on the other, red plastic cups piled high on the chipped table beside it. The room smelled of dust, stale beer and cigarettes. A tangle of shabby furniture was piled haphazardly in one corner, making room for a dance floor on the stained, beige indoor-outdoor carpet. Ash fell from forgotten cigarettes and melted into the dusty carpet as the crowd grew. Soon the room was packed, kids sweating into each other, some holding lit butts overhead, others crowding the keg. Some danced in a circle, their beer falling in little plops as they rocked, stepped and swayed. To my surprise, no one looked at me and said, "What's this kid doing here?" Instead, they wrapped me into the fold as I danced and twirled to a wailing saxophone.

After the party died down, a few of Olaf's closer friends—Caz, Nut (Rachel, so-nicknamed because she hailed from Nutley, New Jersey), Gary and Tom—went back to his room with us. They sat in a circle on the floor, speaking mostly in code I could barely make out—authors and acronyms, professors and assignments. I was starting to nod off on Olaf's bed when the subject turned to gossip—who was dating what senior, who got knocked up—and then they started in on their high school girlfriends. At one point, Caz said, "And then there was Sherry—right, dude?" He looked at Olaf.

"Sheee-it!" Nut yelled. "No, you didn't."

"Oh yeah!" I said, popping up. Here was a subject I finally knew something about. "Sherry! You guys would *love* her."

I thought back to the day I met Sherry, a day I would otherwise never have remembered. It was a typical Saturday with Mom and Dad off to do errands and me, sitting on a patio rocker, wasting time till I could leave for majorette practice. Holding my baton by the grungy, grass-stained end, I flipped it sideways and caught it, then up and catch, up and catch. The buzz of insects, the warm, stagnant air, the forward-and-back of the rocker lulled me into a lazy, eye-staring trance. This early, not quite summer, and it was already too hot to breathe.

"What the . . . " I heard myself yell. From out of nowhere, a little lump of fur had landed in my lap. It was a kitten, a tiny striped kitten purring faintly and burying its head under my chin, pushing upward and into my body, its paws clinging to my damp tee-shirt. "What? And who are you? Where did you come from?"

I'd never held a kitten before. I wrapped one hand under his soft belly and pulled him up to get a better look, which wasn't easy with him clutching so hard. I tore him away, one mini claw at a time, and held him in front of me where he hung, curled into a "c." I peered into his face—so tiny, with eyes that begged for something. His impossibly soft fur was not like my dog's was at all, all curly and thick. I dropped him gently to the ground, ran inside and up the stairs to the kitchen to find the smallest of Mom's bowls, and filled it with milk. I hoped feeding him would make him stay or at least come back from wherever kittens go. At first, he lapped slowly at the milk, peeking suspiciously at me. Then he started drinking for real, ignoring me purposefully and slurping with relish. Late for practice, I jumped on my bike, facing it toward the alley, baton sticking out from my right handlebar. As I looked back, the kitty was still slurping away at the milk, spraying tiny white dots on his yellow whiskers. Even though I doubted Mom would say yes, I hoped I could keep him.

When I got home in the afternoon, Olaf was sitting on the patio across from a girl. She held the kitten in her lap, gently stroking his four-inch back. He purred a soft thanks.

"Holine, this is Sherry," Olaf said.

"Hey," I said. I was more than a little surprised. First a kitten, then a girl with a kitten.

"Hey, Holine," Sherry said, as if she'd known me my whole life.

"But the kitten? How'd he get here?" I asked. "I was sitting here this morning and, like, out of the blue, he jumped on me. I was like, holy crap! Where'd you come from?"

"We brought him home—Sherry and me," Olaf said. "He was wandering around the lake last night, whimpering in the saddest way. Sherry didn't have the heart to leave him."

I was speechless. We are not a cat family, that had long ago been determined. We like dogs, especially cute little ones, like our poodle, Gi-gi. And Mom, well—let's just say she's not an animal person.

"You . . . you guys were at the lake?" I asked.

"Yeah. It was so hot out, so we thought, why not go for a swim?" Olaf said. "Then, all of a sudden, we could hear the poor little guy crying, really sad and lost. So, Sherry couldn't stand it—she scooped him up and now here he is. Aren't you, little guy?" He asked the cat the question like he was talking to a baby, walking over to give him a gentle rub between the ears.

Right then, I just knew Sherry was one of us. Even if you don't love cats, you have to admire someone who rescues one. And, within days, Sherry started calling Mom "Mugsie," Olaf's pet name for her. Sherry teased Dad, calling him "Pugsie," like Mom and Dad were a matched set. She talked to Dad about school, about geometry and physics and how she wanted to go to college in Boston. Dad was a sucker for most girls, especially pretty ones who joked with him and *especially* girls who cared about school. He didn't even seem to mind when she sang along to our protest music, even singing along with her, the two of them a most unlikely duo—Dad, with his square black glasses perched halfway down his nose, his close-cut hair, his dark suits and white dress shirts and Sherry in her tie-dyes and jeans singing along to *Revolution.*

For a while Sherry was at our house all hours of the day—after school, every weekend, even Sunday nights when Dad used to nag us about homework. I was still a little crushed that Olaf and Sherry broke up, just after the prom. He never talked about it. Just . . . one day she was there; the next, she was gone.

"So, this Sherry-girl," Nut said, looking at Olaf. "You were an *item?*"

"Oh yeah," I said. "They even went to the prom together. I still see her at school all the time. She's like a sister."

"Well, that sounds about right," Nut said, and turning to Olaf, she asked. "She's like your sister?"

"Give it a rest, Nut," Olaf said.

"No . . . I meant a sister to *me,*" I said.

"But . . . " Nut started.

Olaf interrupted, "Rach . . . " He glared at Rachel, who, startled at the use of her real name, stopped short. He tilted his head toward me, then, looking straight at Rachel, asked, "Maybe someone had one too many cold ones?"

"Shit," Rachel said. "Sorry, I didn't . . . "

"C'mon, guys," he said. "It's getting late. My little sister here's had a busy day."

The night Olaf came home for Christmas break, Mom made a celebratory dinner of lasagna—Olaf's favorite—and homemade bread. After dinner, while she puttered in the kitchen, Dad, Olaf, and I gathered in the den. Dad scanned the TV dial, settling on Walter Cronkite as usual. He fiddled with the rabbit ears on top of the TV, the screen suddenly flooding with snowy dots, a jarring buzz unsettling the room.

"Where'd I put that damn aluminum foil?" he muttered to himself. He rummaged around under some old newspapers and the *TV Guide* till he finally found a piece, then wrapped it around the antennae till the picture cleared. Satisfied, he settled back into the Barcalounger, he and his chair exhaling a sigh in unison.

"No homework, Jen?" Dad asked.

"In a few, Dad," I said. "I need a little break."

Settling into the rocker's lumpy cushions next to the woodstove, I stared at the colored lights on the Christmas tree, trying to empty my mind of midterm exams, geometry and physics and the countless meaningless formulas just waiting for me to memorize them. Just a few more days and my own Christmas vacation would begin, but all the study-in-waiting was dragging me down, like running laps with weights on my ankles. Unless you were planning to be an engineer or something, like Dad, they seemed a senseless string of letters and numbers I'd intentionally place in my short-term memory bank, where I put everything that I wanted to forget. I couldn't imagine I'd be applying the laws of thermodynamics or electromagnetism to the literature classes I wanted to teach someday.

Poor Dad. Stuck with two bookworms. I stared at him, then at the TV, the familiar image of Walter Cronkite, cut to a group of green-helmeted soldiers clustered closely together, their rifles propped on tripods, the *pop-pop-pop* of warning shots intended to dissuade the resolute enemy that lurked, surreptitiously, in the bush. It could have been last year, or the year before that, or even the year before that—every day, the same reporter, the identical scene. It had only been a year since Cronkite began telling a weary nation that the war in Vietnam was sure to end in stalemate. Yet it dragged on, its sights and sounds so much a part of our lives, we became inured to the noise, the destruction and death.

Just a few miles away where Dad worked at the Air Force base, I wondered what was happening, right then, that was powering the war machine. And how much Dad's work was affected by—or affected—what was unfolding before me. And why he never talked about his service in the Army and his particular job as a serviceman—drawing maps as his plane coasted over Indochina. These were questions I'd learned not to ask. A master of denial and deflection, when it came to war—or any of a number of topics we just *did not discuss*—Dad folded inward, like the maps he had drawn—neat and tidy, their routes hidden within, creased tightly.

The pulpy wood smoke blended with the tree's piney scent, and I breathed it in deeply. Olaf sat, his legs tucked under him on the semi-circular couch, his eyebrows knitted in concentration on his copy of *Slaughterhouse Five*, propped in front of him. I couldn't help but look up at him every so often, back in his usual spot, and I held onto it—the fact that he was there, however temporarily. I moved to the side the knowledge that he'd be gone again in just weeks. Just for one night, the cozy den and Olaf's silent reading comforted me. The past could be present again, if only for the moment. I relaxed for the first time in months.

Then the TV lit up with the words "CBS News" repeated vertically down the screen. In the center in large block letters were the words "SPECIAL REPORT." An official-sounding announcer voice broke in: "Because of the CBS News Special Report which follows, *Mayberry R.F.D.* will not be presented this week but will return next week at its regularly scheduled time over most of these stations. The Draft Lottery: A live report on tonight's picking of the birthdates for the draft. Here at Selective Service Headquarters in Washington is CBS News correspondent Roger Mudd."

I blinked hard. *What?*

Poor Roger Mudd. There he was, propped on the sidelines, a bystander narrating a game of Russian roulette. A bunch of middle-aged white men in identical dark suits and white shirts were gathered in a room. One pulled a blue capsule from a large, oblong glass container, opened it, and loudly declared the date printed on the paper inside. He handed off the paper to a second guy, who stood in front of an enormous rectangular chart and attached the date next to a number. Roger Mudd—who looked pretty shell-shocked himself—told his viewing audience that each number signified the order that men with the chosen birth dates would be drafted and sent to Vietnam. The first date chosen was September 14. That meant any guy with that birthday and born between the years of 1944 and 1950 would go to war first. So—all those guys—they were number one. Number one.

It's pretty ridiculous, but for a moment, all I could think about was our high school football games, all the kids cheering, "We're number one! We're number one!" Then I thought about those boys on our team last year and the year before, the ones who had graduated. The ones whose dads couldn't—or wouldn't—pay for their college tuition. Or the ones some of the teachers declared weren't *college material.* I went down a list in my head and thought about their moms sitting in the stands, cheering along with us about being number one, and how they might feel now about being number one if their kid's birthday was September 14.

Sometimes it takes me a minute to process stuff, so it took me a few beats to catch up. But the guys in suits just kept it up; one took out a blue capsule, yelled out a date, and number two, then number three. But those numbers, they were *people*. And those dates, the ones Roger Mudd mentioned:1950 was one year before Olaf was born.

I looked over at Olaf. Fear, terror, dread—there aren't enough words to describe his horror-filled face. Then I looked at Dad, his expression identical. They knew what I wondered: this would happen again, next year, for boys who were born in 1951, boys like Olaf. We said nothing, just stared in shock like people who happen to come upon a car wreck. As if the lottery wasn't surreal enough, just as the first old guy called out, "February 14 is 004," without warning the video abruptly shifted to commercial: a cartoon Santa gliding down a snowy hill to the tune of "Jingle Bells" on a Norelco electric shaver.

For years, every day after dinner we had watched the war on TV together. Now, it was in our home. Dad cleared his throat, his eyes full. I could not put this new reality aside as I did with my physics formulas. My Olaf would have a draft number. He might really disappear this time. And Dad, who never cried, was crying.

Chapter Four
1970

Late on Friday, March 7, 1970 . . . Inspector Seymour Pine—who led the raid on the Stonewall Inn in June 1969—raided The Snake Pit . . . Among those taken to the Charles Street station was Alfredo Diego Vinales, a twenty-three-year-old Argentinian man with an expired visa; during the mass chaos at the police station, Vinales, terrified of being deported for being homosexual, tried to escape by jumping from an open window to the roof of the next building. Vinales, however, missed the roof and fell onto a fence below, and he was impaled on six of the fence's fourteen-inch iron spikes.

— Spiked on an Iron Fence, *New York Daily News*

    I pulled my patchwork blue raincoat, still stiff and new, from the closet, slipped it on, and looked in the full-length mirror. It was perfect. The coat was cinched neatly, accentuating the tiny waist, its bottom half floating to a bell-shaped A-line, ending precisely at my knees. I was in love with it, so much so that when I slid into the backseat of Dad's new Monte Carlo, I hesitated. I lifted the seatbelt by the buckle, then looked back down at my coat. So crisp and new, I didn't want to wrinkle it. I placed the seatbelt back on the vinyl bench and settled in with a magazine.

    It was Easter break, and although some kids in my class were vacationing someplace warm—Fort Lauderdale and Myrtle Beach and other exotic places I couldn't even envision—

Mom and Dad worked through most of my week off. They were savers who considered vacationing a luxury they couldn't afford. Instead, they salted away Mom's entire salary for Olaf's college tuition. I realized that taking off this one day to take me shopping at the new mall in Syracuse was itself an exception, and not merely a reward for good grades. Mom and Dad sensed my blue mood at the end of a week alone in the quiet house, my first school vacation without Olaf.

Instead of the interstate, Dad took a more leisurely, scenic route, choosing a two-lane highway that curved northwest, alternating through tiny towns and farmland, newly bright green and damp with intermittent rain. I sat behind Mom, *Seventeen's* April 1970 issue opened on my lap, and paged through the ads for shoes and purses and mini dresses, developing my fashion sense before I started browsing the big department stores and the swanky boutiques. For thirty minutes, I immersed myself in the colorful illustrations, admiring the psychedelic-print pants when Dad suddenly jerked the wheel.

The car veered hard toward the right. The brakes screeched; rubber burned and skidded against the pavement. Then, a jolt, a crashing boom, me *inside* the sound, an explosion of shattering glass and the long, grating shriek of metal scraping metal, bending and remolding it against its will, fragments of glass and metal flying like shrapnel, glass chinking and cracking till it slackened to a tinkle, like scraggy icicles that melt and fall against the windows in March. Then, stillness, as sudden as impact. Oppressive silence from outside my head while inside a loud steady *hum* gathered and persisted, staying with me for days afterward.

The impact had propelled me upward and sideways, toward the driver's side. I'd bounced forward and hit the back of Dad's seat, then flew backward with such force that I lurched forward again, then back against the cushion. When I looked down at myself through a slit of light under a veil of clumpy lashes, I noticed that I cradled my left wrist with my right hand. My left arm was useless, and had I not held it, I thought it might crumble to dust. The sleeve of my new coat was spotted crimson. I tasted the metallic warmth of blood on my lips and realized it had run down my face into my mouth from my forehead, which throbbed on the left side, just above the eye that was partially shaded. My coat, a mix of blue fabrics and textures was spattered with dark red splotches across its rectangles. The seatbelt dangled uselessly—from where I could not tell.

From out of the silence a low moan. Then Dad croaked, "Jen, are you all right? Jen?"

"I'm OK, Dad. Take care of Mom," I heard myself say.

Gathering all my strength, I pulled myself upward and looked between the bucket seats, now bent grotesquely in opposite directions. Dad was wedged into his seat at a peculiar angle, pushed forward against the steering wheel, which tilted sideways. Mom was bent under the dash, immovable, surrounded by shards of glass and bent metal, her arms pushed backward, covered in blood. At the sight, I lost my breath and fell backwards against the back-seat cushions.

Time passed. Seconds, minutes or hours—I was not sure—and then a wail of sirens ripped through the downpour.

"Here you go, gently . . . don't get up too fast," an ambulance attendant guided me, holding me tightly under my right elbow, his voice soft and kind. "You OK? You tell me if you feel faint, OK?"

"I'm OK, I think," I said, still unable to see clearly.

"Hang on to me. Just hang on to me," he said, as he gently coaxed me from the back seat. "Think you can sit up?" I nodded. "No stretcher," he yelled to someone crossing the grassy field, several yards from the roadside, where, I realized then, the car had finally stopped. "Now, I gotta cut this so we can see what's happening with that arm, OK?"

"Ok, yeah," I managed. He cut my sleeve upwards from my wrist and tenderly pressed my left arm as I held at a right angle, protecting it with my right.

"Good. Just keeping holding it like that." He guided me toward a running ambulance, helped me into the seat and asked, "Do you think you can slide in?" Since my arms were useless as leverage, I shimmied gradually sideways, edging myself slowly toward the middle of the seat. He climbed in beside me.

"I . . . I can't see so well," I said.

"Yeah. That's a deep cut you got there, but I think the eye will be OK," he said. "Now, I'm gonna just dab it, real soft like . . . here. . . easy . . . easy," he said, as he patted gently at the injury, my forehead throbbing with the beat of my pulse: *thud, thud, thud.* "Yup—that's a nasty one. Lemme get your eyelashes . . . better?"

I nodded.

"Here," he said. "Let's just get this bleeding under control," and he held a soft gauze pad against my forehead, partially covering my left eye.

I looked up to see another attendant wheeling a stretcher. On it, my mother lay motionless, covered by a sheet. A driver helped the attendant slide her into the back of another ambulance, and then she was gone. I was certain that she was dead.

"Mom!" I cried. "Where are they taking her?"

"We're all going to Upstate, don't worry," he said. "We've already got your dad in the back. That's your Dad who was driving, right?"

"Yeah," I said, and rested my head against the seatback. Sirens whined and moaned as the ambulance turned into the highway and began a frenzied drive through stoplights, other traffic at a standstill. Trees, stores, people, cars blurred together as we blew through the suburbs, the speed pushing me back in my seat. Every so often, the attendant bent down and asked me, "How you doin' now, kid?" shaking me from the dream state I wandered in and out of.

And then, somehow I was in a hospital bed in a big private room, white everywhere—walls, sheets, blanket, sink. I had on one of those hospital gowns—white cotton with little blue triangles—that someone had tied across the back of my neck. A nurse scurried in and out. She might have taken my temperature and my blood pressure; she might have held my good wrist to measure my pulse. She covered me with the blanket. I was in and out, the shock like undertow, submerging me under water once . . . and again.

"My mom and dad?" I asked. "Where are my mom and dad?"

"I'll check for you honey," she said. "Now, just rest your head back."

I waited, the thud in my head growing worse as my left eye began to sting, as if something sharp was tearing into the skin above it. It could have been minutes or hours later, a doctor swept in and was suddenly at my bedside.

"Well, what do we have here?" he said cheerfully, as if I was some kind of nifty experiment he couldn't wait to conduct.

"My mom and dad?" I asked. "Where's my mom and dad?"

"Your dad's OK," he said. "We're just doing some x-rays, but he's up and around. You'll see him later."

"But Mom?" I said. "Where's Mom?"

"Hmmm," he answered. "I haven't seen your mom. I'll check for you, though. Now, let's get after this cut."

The nurse was back, sitting me up straighter in bed and assisting the doctor, who numbed my eye with something that stung and burned, smelling sharply of rubbing alcohol. The antiseptic smell, the ammonia-scrubbed room, and stale, dead air made my head swim, and I felt myself fade, on the verge of slipping away. Steady hands caught my shoulders, coaxing me back toward the pillow.

"Deep breaths," she said. "Try to relax."

Then the doctor leaned in and slowly stitched me back together, each stroke preceded by a tug and sting, while the pulsing around my eye socket continued its rhythmic ache.

"Good as new!" the doctor exclaimed and smiled broadly as he finished. "Well . . . almost."

"What you mean . . . almost?"

"Well . . . it'll be a tad more *colorful* for a while—you're gonna have a nasty shiner around that cut," he said, and then, reacting to the rising alarm he must have seen in my face, added, "Don't worry, now . . . the white of your eye is blood-red—I know, it's scary—but no cause for concern. Just broken blood vessels. It'll heal in no time." He patted my hand, then said, "Now, let's get an x-ray of that arm."

The nurse helped me into a wheelchair and rolled me to x-ray, where the technician sat me on a platform and gently placed my arm on a shiny metal plate. Then he scurried into a little booth on the side of the room.

"Hold still," he called out, and I heard a *click* and *swoosh*. Then he was back beside me, gingerly picking up my arm with both hands and gently maneuvering it into an awkward angle back on the shiny surface. "Sorry—it'll only be a minute. One more time. Hold it," he said. The *click* and *swoosh* again, and then he said, "OK. Rest." I picked up my left arm with my right, holding it together, fearing it might come apart.

"You can sit back in the wheelchair now," he said, swooping in beside me to guide me back into the chair.

Minutes later, he showed me a murky gray image of my wrist and arm: shattered bone expressed as black slashes where white should have been. Wheeled to another room, I was half aware as a new doctor wrapped my arm, molding it into a hard cast.

Somehow, I was back in the original room alone. I dozed, waited, dozed again, each time waking and wondering for a moment if the sounds in my head were real. I still hadn't seen Dad or Mom. I still hadn't cried.

I must have dozed. I blinked my good eye open, and there was Olaf—or I thought it was Olaf, unless I'd dreamed him there, sitting in a chair by my bed and leaning over me, red-eyed, like he'd been crying.

"Olaf," I said, and he moved toward me. Then I started to cry too.

"Oh, no, no, no," he said, his eyes filling with tears. "Your poor little eye. Don't cry now. I'm here."

"But Mom? And Dad—where's Dad?" I said. "No one will tell me anything."

"Dad's here," Olaf said. "He'll be OK."

"Mommy?" I asked.

"They took her to Crouse," he said, and then, when I sat up abruptly, panicked, he continued. "She'll be OK. It's just going to take time. Lie back now." He brushed away the gooey hair that had fallen forward toward the gash over my eye. "You should rest."

"It . . . it was . . ." I started to explain, but I dropped back on the pillow. Olaf took my hand.

Weeks of recovery followed, with Mom making little strides forward, then weeping into her pillow on bad days. She left the hospital after a week's stay, but the broken shoulder, a shattered heel, and cracked ribs made mobility difficult. She'd had stitches, tiny lines sketched on her face, like the secondary streets on a roadmap. Scores of miniscule glass particles had wedged in her forehead and cheek, so many that for months she pulled out one tiny fragment at a time as it finally pushed its way through her tender skin. As days became weeks, she grew more and more frustrated with all she could not do—and would not be able to do, not for months. Her sisters rallied, each of my aunts taking shifts hovering over Mom—washing her hair, cooking her meals, lifting her spirits. In a sizable Italian family like ours, the women were the caretakers while the men averted their eyes, burying their heads in practical matters—punching the clock, paying the gas bill, mowing the lawn, unclogging the drain—and in the process, burying their feelings.

Mom, Dad and I moved like phantoms through a silent house, our conversation, our music, our TV—muted and irregular. We folded ourselves inward, not daring to look directly at each other, each of us a trigger for the others' post-traumatic stress with our stitched-together foreheads, our plum-colored welts and plaster casts. Whenever Dad glanced my way, even for a moment, his face dissolved in sadness, reminding me just how broken I must've looked. Our own cuts and bandages were bearable. Seeing each other's pain was not.

In May, Olaf came home from college for the summer, and the house sprung open, as if the life in his eyes was transmittable, his rosy, flawless skin a promise of healing. The timing of his arrival was synchronized with the landscape: the lilacs' green buds burst in a spray of purple, the maples turned from pale chartreuse to deep, vigorous emerald. Olaf's spirit—his face bright with expectation—reminded us what could be, as he chattered excitedly about college, the role he gotten—Schroeder, of course—in the production of *You're a Good Man, Charlie Brown,* his gig as a nighttime disc jockey on the college radio station.

With his stereo back in place, from a speaker propped in the window facing our hideout on the roof, guitars seesawed the introduction to his favorite new album, *Déjà vu*—and it *was* déjà vu, the house full of Olaf, as if he'd never left. Immersed in his incandescent buoyancy, Mom, Dad and I leaned into healing. The red blotch in my eye faded to tiny red islands in a white sea; my sawed-off cast was replaced by a new one that stopped mid-forearm, freeing my elbow, and in the process, making my movements instinctive, making me familiar to myself again.

About a week after he'd come home, one morning Olaf sat at his usual spot at the kitchen bar staring into his Rice Krispies, barely taking a bite. Usually ravenous in the morning, he pushed his bowl across the table, the little kernels within having coalesced into a soggy sandbar in a pond of white. He retreated to the front porch, where he skulked around, sometimes pacing the twenty-foot sidewalk, back-and-forth, back-and-forth. When the mail truck appeared at the Linden corner, he sat on a porch rocker, his eyes fixed on the mailman as he made his way—stopping at each house along the street, hesitating, searching his bag, clustering envelopes and magazines. Finally reaching our house, the mailman handed a pile of mail to Olaf.

"Lovely day, isn't it?" he said, but Olaf was already thumbing through the pile until he found the envelope, return-addressed "Utica College." He peeked under the fold, then stashed the letter in his pocket and motioned me to follow him to his room.

"Whad'ya get?" I asked.

"Grades," he said, hanging his head and shaking it slowly, side-to-side. "Ugh! Public relations!—what a crock!"

"Sorry?" I asked.

"My stupid major," he said. "I *hate* it. Business . . . marketing"

"Damn," I said. "What'll you do now?"

"I'm getting out," he said.

"What?" I asked. "Out? Not out of college . . . Dad will have a cow! And . . . the draft!"

"No—geez, I haven't lost my mind! Olaf said. "My major—I'm changing to English. I've already applied to Geneseo. Starting this fall." *Geneseo.* So much farther away. Olaf peeked up at me, measuring my reaction.

"Aaaa . . . do Mom and Dad know?"

Olaf thought a minute. He ignored my question. "Ugh! And accounting!" Olaf wailed, like sitting through accounting class was akin to electric shock treatments.

"You flunked?" I asked.

"Oh, I flunked all right," he said. "I couldn't do even one problem on the exam. Not one. So, I wrote a poem instead."

"A *poem?*" I asked, but when I imagined the professor opening Olaf's blue book, I couldn't help laughing. "A poem. Are you insane?"

"At least it was *about* accounting . . . " he said. "Wanna hear it?"

This oughta be good, I thought. I nodded, but I couldn't help thinking about what Dad would do if he knew Olaf had written a poem in his accounting blue book.

"Dear Professor Sweatervest," Olaf began, his voice taking on a regal, clipped tone, with just a hint of British accent.

> *It's my duty to inform you,*
> *Despite my best efforts,*
> *In pursuit of accounting*
> *I'll never be expert.*

> *So today I pronounce myself*
> *Czar of stupidity*
> *In matters of assets,*
> *Margins, liquidity.*

> *A failure am I at the*
> *Study of equity,*
> *While ledgers and interest*
> *Bring me no levity.*

> *And so my exam*
> *I've transformed into poetry,*
> *My portfolio diversified*
> *From all that you know of me.*

"You didn't!" I doubled over, tears rolling down my face by the time he'd finished. "Impressive," I croaked through my howls.

"Yeah," Olaf said. He smiled a mischievous elf smile. "Think I should recite it for Dad?"

"Yeah, right," I said. "Let me know so I can bail first."

But then a strange thing happened. When Olaf broke the news—all of it, even his transfer plans—and handed over the grade report to Dad, Dad just said something like, "Sometimes finding out what we don't want helps us discover what we do want." I was pretty blown away when he said that, but then again, Dad was different in those months after the accident. He was stuck there, submerged in the idea that all three of us could have died. Not in a bad way or, like, mired in some revolving, morbid nightmare, but he—well, all of us, really—knew something we hadn't been able to know: that a few critical moments had turned our lives into a timeline of events, and each event fell into one of two categories: "before," and "after." And in this new "after," our bloodied and bandaged eyes, despite our clouded vision, could suddenly see with a clarity what we otherwise would not have known.

One perfect June evening—bright sunshine, 75 degrees, no humidity and the slightest warm breeze—Mom was feeling better, energized by the gorgeous day and not wanting to waste it. She was finally on her feet again—although still self-conscious about her scars and the limp she couldn't control, still wearing these ugly corrective shoes the doctor insisted on.

"Hey Hon," she said to Dad, "How 'bout you drive us over to the concert tonight?"

"Love to," he said. He grinned and nodded at me. He'd been waiting for her to suggest it, hoping that getting her out of the house would bring her fully back to life. And Olaf, who never stopped performing, loved it when we came to his concerts. He'd be so happy to see Mom there again.

"Wanna come, Jen?" she asked.

"Sure," I said, finishing up the second of the long braids that lined the side of my face. I'd just gotten my second cast off, and though my arm was shriveled and scaly, I was finally starting to do all these normal things that seem really easy till you can't do them.

The concert was a weekly event at the picturesque Ilion Town Park, under a bandstand with a sloping, pointed roof and encircled by a painted white railing. For a couple of years, Olaf played percussion—drums and xylophones and claves—as he had in high school band. When those instruments became too easy for him, Olaf started practicing the old piccolo, swiping it from under my bed where I'd hidden it after I quit band abruptly in eighth grade. I didn't even know he'd taken it, when, one day I was in my room plunking away at the Smith-Corona, and, out of nowhere, I heard the famous piccolo solo from *Stars and Stripes Forever*. I looked out the door and there was Olaf with his band hat on—the kind with the little plume and the black chin strap—marching in time down the hall, somehow smiling while he played—not easy to do while you're blowing over a hole. How he learned it so fast, I'll never know. I clapped like a maniac.

Dad, Mom and I piled into the Monte Carlo—the new one, exactly like the old one—that Dad had picked up just that week. Dad steered the car east onto the highway. There was this one spot—four corners with a traffic light—on what was otherwise a high-speed highway. Dad was always cautious, but never more so than after the accident. As we approached the light, we heard the wail of a siren and saw the flashing light of a police car up ahead.

"Oh, no!" Mom said. "Looks like an accident."

I leaned toward the middle to look out past the dash, a flashback of flying glass shards and the scraping of torn metal passing through my head. Then, as Dad coasted into a stop at the red light, we all saw it at once: Olaf's car on the side of the road, its backend bent upward at a right angle.

"My God!" Mom screamed. I lost my breath, my heartbeat.

"No!" I cried. "Oh God. No!"

"Stay here!" Dad yelled. He pulled the car over, jumped out and sprinted down the street.

"Mama, I have to . . . " I began. I unbuckled my seatbelt.

"Jen, stay here," she said, both of us straining to see.

Mom whispered a mantra of desperate prayers. "Oh, Jesus, please dear God, please dear God, make him be all right, make him be all right." I sat shaking, my hand on the door handle, fighting the overpowering urge to run.

Then we saw him: Olaf, up ahead, walking slowly along the shoulder, his head down, his hand over his mouth.

"Oh, thank God," Mom whimpered.

But he didn't look like Olaf. He moved slowly, floating like a ghost on the roadside, his face deathly white, his eyes dark as storm clouds.

I jumped out of my seat and ran toward him.

"Here, honey," I called. "We're here!"

He looked up. And for just a moment, I swear he didn't recognize me.

Chapter Five
1973

Last weekend, the Board of Trustees of the American Psychiatric Association approved a change in its official manual of psychiatric disorders. "Homosexuality per se," the trustees voted, should no longer be considered a 'psychiatric disorder;' it should be defined instead as a 'sexual orientation disturbance.'"

—The Issue is Subtle: The Debate is Still On, *The New York Times*

When my friends and I rolled up on the parking lot of Lock, Stock and Barrel, the place was already buzzing, the band's thumping drum in the distance competing against the blare of car radios, all tuned to WOUR—"the Rock of Central New York," "Smoke on the Water" blasting from cobbled-together stereo speakers beside bobble-head dolls on car back dashes. Kids lined the steps of the fire escapes, mingled in open convertibles and clustered on truck flatbeds where pungent smoke drifted up in little clouds. One girl, her legs dangling off a tailgate, threw back her wild hair and laughed uproariously as her friend retrieved the wayward flip-flop which had slipped off her foot and landed in a mud puddle.

I climbed the creaky wooden steps, well-worn from the years that Lock, Stock and Barrel had been a restaurant catering to the early-bird-special crowd. By the time I reached the top, the music boomed at full volume in my ears; the rank smell of old beer that had seeped into the cracked wooden floor filled my nostrils. The two doors leading out to the fire escapes were open, the only source of semi-fresh air on a clammy mid-July night.

I scanned the room, and saw him right away: the baseball coach, Paul, with whom I'd exchanged flirtatious glances at our summer playground jobs. He was dancing with someone I'd seen before—a pretty, black-haired girl with huge eyes. Quickly looking away, I pulled at my halter top, straightened my shoulders, and assumed the most carefree expression I could muster. Relieved to see some friends from high school in a crowd of kids nearby, I rushed to greet them, trying to ignore my sinking stomach.

"Whoa!" Jim, a friend whom I hadn't seen in months took both my hands. "You look amazing! That tan!"

"My job," I said, "For the Rec Department. I'm outside all day, every day."

"Whatever it is," he said, "It's working for you. You certainly grew up," he said, a little creepily, and though I took his hand when he offered it, I backed away just the same. Just then, I felt someone come up behind me. When I turned, Paul was already squeezing in next to me.

"Hey, Jim!" he said, but he was looking at me. Then he turned, bent toward me and whispered, "I was hoping you might be here. C'mon, let's go dance."

From that point on, neither Paul nor I talked to anyone else. We didn't dance with anyone else. We just danced . . . and danced and danced and danced. We stopped only once, taking a break on the fire escape—finally empty—where Paul kissed me once . . . then again—kisses like memories, belonging only to us, regardless who we'd kissed before or who we might ever kiss again. Around one a.m., the place began to clear out, and I said good-bye to my friends, choosing to ride home with Paul.

The events of summer flashed like July fireflies that, try as I might, could not be captured in a jar. Without warning, all the days that Paul and I had spent together—inseparable as we were after that first night on the dance floor—were done. I sat alone, waiting, dangling my feet off the deck overlooking Paul's backyard. I stared at his mother's flower gardens that lined the yard on both sides, the bright yellow sunflowers, magenta and powder blue hydrangeas, and blood red hibiscus mocking me with their cheerfulness. On either side of me, large terra cotta pots overflowed with cascading purple petunias and a newly-purchased orange mum, its countless buds about to flower. In the distance, from behind the garage I heard Paul's father call out, "That everything?"

"Just about, Dad," Paul answered, then jogged up the sidewalk, up the deck steps, smiling toward me as he passed by and into the house. Moments later, he re-emerged with an oversized athletic bag, a baseball bat protruding from one side, his first baseman's glove hanging off the end. After loading it in the trunk, he returned to the deck, slower this time.

Paul's dad peered around the side of the garage. "Going to gas up," he called. He backed up the car, gravel popping and cracking across the alley. When the car turned the corner, Paul took my hands in his.

"This is it, I guess," he said, and drew me closer to him. "Here, take this." He handed me a plastic Catholic scapular attached to a tiny sliver ring. "Keep it in your pocket." Silent tears escaped the corners of my eyes, and he gently brushed them away. I focused on the tiny twin beauty marks over his lip, the arch of his eyebrows, the gentle upward curve of his nose, expressive green eyes that drooped sadly.

"Hey," he said soothingly. "Columbus weekend, right?"

"I know," I said. "I'm already counting the weeks."

He bent toward me, and brushing the hair from my forehead, kissed me there, then my eyes, one . . . then the other . . . as if his kisses could dry my tears. Just then his father's car rounded the corner. The car horn blared. Paul broke away, walked toward the car, then turned and smiled weakly, raising his hand in a half-hearted wave.

A week later, Mom and Dad helped me pack the car before they dropped me off at my new dorm. At the top of the bag full of school supplies was a box of scented stationery, 100 sheets of pale pink parchment with matching envelopes. Now, I'd have double the letters to write.

The air was eternally thick with smoke. Residue left a permanent grime on the hallway walls. Hazy cones of light shone from the dim bulbs of the corridor. As I walked across the carpet, once variegated and now flattened to a dull gray, ash wafted up, mingling with years of dust. Cigarettes, worn upholstery, incense—the stale, leftover odor latched onto my hair and clothes. Music boomed from every door. *Statesboro Blues* melded into *Layla* as I walked past one room, then the next. From move-in day through my entire freshman year, an echo of the dorm followed me wherever I went, the music in my head even when it wasn't playing, the scents embedded into the threads of my jeans, into my very cells.

I lay on a thin mattress beside the window and looked out at the snowstorm, layers of white in all directions. Ever since I'd returned to college after Thanksgiving vacation, the weather *did not stop*. Back home, the snow fell. Here, it swept sideways in heavy swaths, so thick I couldn't make out the Ontario Lakeshore only feet from my dorm room. The wind whooshed and whistled against windows that rattled non-stop, the sound constant and unyielding, our special brand of white noise. Lying back on the flimsy dorm mattress, watching the snow collect on the ledge, I could still conjure the smell of Paul's sunbaked skin after a day on the playground, still feel his fingers—thick, coated with a dusting of infield dirt—intwined with mine as he walked me home. I shifted my gaze from the snow cascading under the streetlamp's jaundiced eye to the wobbly desk barely supporting a massive pile of books. It seemed to grow taller with each passing day, especially at night when it loomed in dark shadow, one giant vertical blotch. Anthropology, Archaeology, Psychology, Advanced Algebra. Each course had its own language with so many new words; each class was like our high school field trip to Montreal, only without my French-English dictionary. Every day, although I watched and listened and took careful notes, I felt like an intruder waiting to be discovered. Behind in my reading, I'd dug myself a deep hole.

I wrestled myself from under my quilt, then pulled it off the bed and wrapped myself in it, dragged it and myself to the desk. My dorm desk chair was straight and hard, so it was a pretty good bet I wouldn't nod off, no matter how much of a drag "Chapter Eight: Classical and Operant Conditioning" happened to be. I sighed into my desk chair, opened my psychology textbook, and adjusted the bendable desk lamp over it. I read: "In the case of classical conditioning, the focus is on what happens prior to a response. We begin with a stimulus, one that will trigger a specific response." I began mindlessly coloring chapter eight's pages with a yellow highlighter. My eyes slid across the words as my mind wandered. It hadn't been that long ago since Olaf screwed up that semester, and I mean, if he could mess up—and let's face it, he was so much smarter than I'd ever be—no wonder I was in over my head. The difference was he pretty much flunked on purpose.

Self-destruction would not help me, though. I was already in an Education program, my choice alone. Writing a limerick wouldn't cut it; nothing would get me out of the classes I was taking, all requirements. I looked down at my book, page 268, and read, "Vicarious classical conditioning, as it is called, occurs when we observe the emotional reactions of a person to a stimulus . . . " I tried to recall classical conditioning, classical conditioning . . . that's what I got for letting myself daydream my way through pages, my highlighter squeaking yellow across lines I hadn't even tried to understand. I paged back to the beginning and was about to start over when the phone rang.

"Hey, Holine," Olaf's voice on the other end could not have been more welcome. "How's it going?"

"Oh my God," I said. "Olaf!"

"What's up, kiddo?" he asked.

"Oh, man. These classes," I said. "They're killing me."

"Yeah, I know," he said. "Freshman year. It's the *worst*."

"You got that right," I said. "Archaeology. Anthropology. What does any of this have to do with teaching English?"

"I gotta be honest," he said. "Not much."

"And this stupid psych test tomorrow," I groaned. "So much reading."

"I know . . . " he said. "But I know you: when you put your mind to something . . . "

"And the weather here!" I yelled, interrupting. "We thought we had winter! *This* is winter. It just . . . it snows *sideways*, all the time. And it's so cold!" Now I was up and pacing, turning one way, then the other as the phone cord wound around my back. "They put up ropes! *Ropes!*"

"Ropes?" he asked. "What the hell for?"

"They have these fence posts," I shrieked, "along *all* the walkways, strung with ropes. Because the wind—it never stops whipping sideways."

"Sheesh."

"Yeah. Because we can't even walk!" I moaned. "It's ridiculous! We have to pull ourselves forward with ropes."

"Sounds brutal," he said, "but, it's almost over. Less than four weeks to break."

"Yeah, that's what I keep telling myself—only four more weeks," I said. "Anyway, what's up with you? I hear music and voices in the background. You at a party?"

"No. Just having a couple of people over," he said. "Lemme go in the bedroom, so we can talk."

A creak, a door closed, the music moved farther away.

"So," he said. "I was talking to my friends here, and they thought I should call you."

"Why? What's up?" I asked. "You sound funny."

"Oh no—I'm fine," Olaf said. "It's just . . . I have something I've been wanting to tell you. Something pretty important." Olaf cleared his throat.

"You're scaring me a little." I untangled myself from the cord and sat back down on the desk chair.

"Well, I should've told you before now, but . . . I don't know . . . " he began.

"You know you can tell me anything," I said.

"Yeah, I know. It's just . . . it's about me," he said.

"You sure you're OK?" I asked. His tone had become serious, so *not* Olaf. I braced myself for bad news. Maybe he was sick. Or transferring again, even farther away.

"Yeah, yeah. Good actually," he said. "But . . . um, do you remember me and Mom arguing? In high school?"

"I mean . . . I guess, a little."

"Before Sherry," he said. "Remember?"

"I figured she was just being all *Mom*," I said, "putting herself in the middle."

"Yeah," he said. "Well, she *was* being all Mom, but it's . . . it was because, of . . . well, of how I am."

"What do you mean?" I asked.

"I mean, I don't . . . I don't have relationships with girls," he said, his voice lowered.

"I know. It's been years since you had a girlfriend, but . . ."

"Well, there's another reason for that, an actual reason," he began. "It's because I don't date girls," he whispered the last part, as if there was anyone else to hear. "I'm gay," he said, his voice cracking.

"Gay," I repeated it, tried to take it in. The word spoken aloud like a splash of cold water on my face before I was totally awake.

"Yes. Gay," he said. "I've been wanting to tell you. I'm sorry I waited so long. I just didn't want anything to come between us," he said.

"Come between *us?*"

"I know . . . but that's just it. We're so close," he began, "and I want us to stay that way."

"Olaf—how could we *not?*"

"I know, but it's important that you—you, of all people—that you know. You're too important to me to keep secrets."

"I never want secrets between us either," I said.

"Earlier, well, you were young. I didn't want you drawn into the drama—with Mom and everything. I mean, she's known for a while."

"Dad?" I asked, in an almost whisper.

"Hell no!" he said. "She wouldn't hear of it."

"I should've guessed she'd keep it from him. But you know . . . maybe on some level, I knew all along," I said. "Maybe he does too."

"You knew?" Olaf asked.

"Yeah, well . . . I didn't actually say it to myself," I said. "But, listen. This is the thing: you're my Olaf. That's all that matters to me."

"I'm so relieved to hear you say that," Olaf said. "I needed so much for you to be OK with it. It's been killing me."

"I just want you to be happy," I said. "You're happy, right?"

"Happier right now—this moment—than I've been—like, ever." His voice broke, and I realized that he was crying. Then I realized that I was crying.

"Why are we crying?" I asked. We both laughed then, even as the tears were running down my face.

"It feels so good to finally say it!" he said, and then, "You're . . . well, thanks, Holine. I love you." His words felt to me like the hug I knew so well, thin arms around my shoulders, drawing me in.

"I love you, too," I said. "See you soon—Christmas!"

"Four weeks!" he said, his voice bursting with joy.

I hung up the phone and went into the hall. All was quiet. Nothing to say, no one to say it to, not that I would talk to anyone about our conversation. I walked to the dark study lounge and sunk into the rickety couch, nubs of worn upholstery on the armrest chafing against my skin. The wind whipped against the

52

window as the pounding snow continued, continuous streams of white under the solitary lamppost—the weather the one constant in my new, temporary home. As I stared out the window, a half hour became an hour, then an hour and half. I rose reluctantly, turned back to my room, slipped on my nightgown and went to bed.

Too much awake, I rolled one way, then another, twisting in my sheets. I turned the pillow over and fluffed it up. The conversation with Olaf played over and over in my head, a tape on a loop. I thought about how it must have been for him, knowing and holding on to his secret, worrying and wondering how—or *if*—he should tell his family. The hints that shaded so much of our early life seemed at the time like ordinary growing pains. Now I pictured them as a progression, a line of signposts leading always to this place, this moment.

One particular incident, long ago forgotten, flashed to the foreground. It was one of those endless childhood days during summer break. It had rained nonstop, and Olaf and I, sick of leaning over the Monopoly board while TV game shows played continuously in the background, had looked for something interesting to do. I sat across the couch from him and opened *Little House in the Big Woods* on my lap. Olaf had retrieved the mail and was leafing through *Life* magazine. About halfway through the pages, I noticed Olaf had stopped short and pulled the magazine closer. I strained to see over the top, wondering what could be so compelling. I caught a glimpse of a few men standing in the shadows of a darkened room, a mural behind them almost their mirror image. Olaf tilted the magazine so I couldn't see, his eyebrows scrunched together in concentration.

"What 'cha reading?" I asked.

"Nothing," he said. But I could tell: whatever he was reading was interesting enough that he'd assumed that intense look, the one that dared me not to bother him. Still, it wasn't like him not to share what was in the magazine. I grabbed for it.

"*Stop it!* Leave me alone!" he cried, snatching up the magazine and running to his room. He slammed the door, and I heard the skeleton key click inside the lock. He'd never locked me out before.

I had to wait several days until he was out of the house to finally get the chance to sneak into his room, a room so small a twin bed, a nightstand and a three-drawer dresser barely fit within it. It was not exactly a room with many good hiding places. Under his bed I found only Baby Ruth wrappers, an empty Pez dispenser, a pair of battered drumsticks, and the abandoned, deflated football he'd gotten for Christmas and had never thrown once. No magazine.

I checked his bottom drawer, where junk mingled among his treasures—stray playing cards bent at the corners, music books, flash cards and vocabulary workbooks, a box of crayon nubs and an old cigar box filled with a gold St. Christopher medal and a cat's eye ring, some gum wrapper chains, his Communion catechism, a Polaroid of us on a picnic and a few silver dollars. There was so much stuff that the drawer got stuck when I tried to close it. Then I realized why: there was a magazine jammed behind the drawer.

Sitting on the floor, my back against his bed frame, I found the article with the scary men in the picture. *Homosexuality in America*. I read: "These brawny young men in their leather caps, shirts, jackets and pants are practicing homosexuals . . . part of what they call the 'gay world,' which is actually a sad and often sordid world . . . "

I snapped the magazine shut and tucked it back behind the drawer. I didn't know what some of the words meant, but I *did* know "sad" and "sordid." I consciously slid the memory in the back of the drawer along with the magazine.

I'd suppressed that episode for so many years, and now, as I turned over in bed, I wondered how much that article may have scared him, how it might have made him withdraw in secrecy and shame. I tried to recall the fights between him and Mom, when they happened, where I was, what I was doing, and why I was so oblivious. Overcome with guilt, I realized how much he'd endured alone, even while I understood the secret he'd kept from me was yet another way he'd chosen to protect me.

Giving up on sleep, I sat up in bed. I leaned over the bed and pulled various volumes from the bookshelf beside it—an old book of poetry Olaf had given me on my sixteenth birthday, a scrapbook full of newspaper clippings—our names on Honor Roll lists and band photos from the evening paper—and then, at the end of the shelf, a photo album. I pulled it onto the bed and switched on the light over my head. Gently turning the pages, the memories flooded back—Olaf and I seated side-by-side at a picnic table, watermelon triangles on paper plates in front of us; me on a swing at the beach and Olaf reaching up to give me a push; the Ilion Band under the bandstand, and in the front row, a mini-Olaf face under a plumed hat. Toward the end of the album were the photos from Olaf's Senior Ball: one photo after another of Olaf and Sherry—in a flowing white gown, daisies strewn in her hair. Olaf in a silvery gray suit, a white carnation pinned to his lapel. And finally, one of Olaf and Sherry, taken just before they left for the Ball: Olaf's arm crooked awkwardly around Sherry's shoulders, his clenched-teeth smile and downcast, miserable eyes. It was the face of a boy just becoming a man, desperate to run, to slip into his authentic skin.

And I, a fourteen-year-old, eager to see only the romance of a senior ball, had missed it.

Chapter Six
1976

Thousands of homosexuals yesterday paraded along the Avenue of the Americas, from Greenwich Village to Central Park, in the seventh annual march for homosexuals' rights. Aided by cool breezes in the 90-degree weather, the demonstrators, carrying placards and waving banners, made the 52-block march in slightly more than an hour. Organizers of the march said its purpose was twofold, to show support for the passage of local, state and Federal homosexual civil rights legislation and to press for repeal of legislation that prohibits or limits sexual conduct between consenting adults in private.

Thousands Join in March for Homosexuals' Rights, *The New York Times*

I squealed my wheels out of the Kennedy Middle School parking lot, opened the driver's side window all the way, and turned up the radio to an insane volume, me and Stevie Nicks singing with abandon, "Dreams unwind; love's a state of mind." I'd been mentally pacing all day, my brain the equivalent of a lion skulking from side-to-side within its cage. It was finally Friday of a week that felt like a month, and I was driving to visit Olaf at his new Geneseo apartment, my first trip completely on my own. And it was spring—finally spring!—after a winter that was one long lake-effect blizzard. This particular, fabulous Friday, the sun shone at last, and I actually felt it for the first time since last summer: warmth toasting the skin of my left arm as it rested across the window's edge.

I wanted a beer, some pizza, the noise and hum of adult talk. I wanted a dark bar with a good juke box and packs of Winstons stacked in a vending machine. I wanted to shop, to buy something I shouldn't. But mostly I wanted to talk with Olaf about student teaching. He was a teacher now, a real one; he would know how to make things better. Much as I wanted a break from school, what I needed more was to talk about it.

Whizzing past farms and fields at 70 miles an hour, I occasionally glimpsed the shoreline of Lake Ontario, my backyard for the last four years. I realized I had never taken the time to fathom its enormity. It was massive, reaching halfway across the state, its shoreline piled with hundreds of thousands of round rocks polished smooth by rumbling gray water. I passed Red Creek and Wolcott, Sodus and Webster. Traffic picked up as I reached Rochester, the city beckoning me away from the backwoodsy life of my students, a life where I just didn't fit in. The closer I got to the city, the faster I drove, the more light-hearted and free I felt. By the time I turned toward Geneseo and Olaf's home with his new boyfriend, Ted, I was downright buoyant, pounding the wheel in rhythm to the radio, still cranked to the max.

"Holine!" Olaf ran out the door and was beside the car before I could even turn off the ignition. "You made it!" Like a shirt on a scarecrow, a flimsy, over-washed t-shirt hung on him, untucked over jeans worn white at the knees. The familiar *click-click-click* of his scuffed-thin flip-flops, the thick swoop of shiny brown hair across his forehead, forest green eyes flashing with delight—just the sight of him was like a deep cleansing breath. "Oh, Holine!" he called again, opening the door for me and giving me the hug I'd needed for weeks—maybe months. He took my face in his hands, his eyes dancing into mine, and said, "You're here. You're really here!" He opened the trunk, pulled out the beat-up, orange Samsonite, and swinging his left arm around my waist, led me to the door.

The apartment was all Olaf. It smelled of coffee and new kittens. A rickety piano, front and center, was strewn with yellowed sheet music, pages left open in mid-play. A 12-inch black-and-white TV perched on a Formica-topped stand, rabbit ears pointing in crazy diverging directions, aluminum foil wrapped around their tips. The battered coffee table was piled with student essays, some laced with Olaf's red scrawl. Records spanned the longest wall in the living room, stacked side-by-side between two gargantuan speakers. Olaf gave me a quick tour down a hallway to the one bedroom. In it were only a dresser and bed, a tower of books beside it. There were two photos on the dresser, one of me at my high school graduation, and one of Ted. I picked up the one of Ted to get a better look.

"That's my Teddy," Olaf said. "Cute, right?"

"Cute isn't the word . . . he's a fox! Adorable, just like I pictured him." Teddy had brown, slightly tousled hair, warm brown eyes, a straight nose and an impossibly symmetrical face. He cuddled a spotted kitten between his neck and shoulder. A sweet, gentle soul—that was my impression.

"I wish you could've met him," Olaf said. "Too bad he had a family thing this weekend."

"Next time," I assured him. "Later, in the summer."

"Besides, this weekend, I have big plans for you! Tonight, we're going to Geneseo's *best* restaurant for dinner!" He laughed, "Granted, there are only two restaurants in town, but it's actually pretty good. And tomorrow, we're going to a high school play! Won't that be just terrific?" As he said this, he feigned super excitement, clapping his hands together, his eyes flashing convincingly.

"Oh, man," I groaned. "Not more school!"

"Holine, we *have* to go. I promised my kids," he said. "But, you'll see. Some of them can actually act. And sing!" he said.

Oh, great, I thought: a *musical*.

"They're not half bad," Olaf said. "Honest." And I could tell by his bright, encouraging eyes, he believed it.

The restaurant was as nice as he described—scrubbed clean linoleum, white tablecloths, solitary candles blinking in the dim light, our table in a semi-private nook. The aroma of sweet, simmered tomatoes and basil reminded me of Mom's kitchen. As we sipped Chardonnay and nibbled at our lasagna, Olaf said, "So, tell me about school."

"Ugh," I sighed. "School. I tell you; I don't know how you do it. It's really not going well. I mean, I had this idea that I'd be teaching stuff I love. Instead, I feel more like a hall monitor, or no—an attendant in a psych ward."

"Well, you *do* have middle-schoolers," he said. "They're a species unto themselves."

"You don't know the half of it," I said. "My first day?"

"Oh, no," he said. "Bad news?"

"Insane," I said. "I get there, and my master teacher basically says 'Follow me,' so I do: right into a fifty-student study hall in the cafeteria. Fifty seventh and eighth graders. *Fifty*."

"Sheesh," Olaf said. "Some start."

"So, she takes the roll," I began, "and then she looks at me and says, 'I just gotta run get my mail . . . be right back.' And she leaves me! Leaves me, without even a seating chart."

"Oh no . . . she didn't," Olaf said, shaking his head.

"Oh, yeah," I said. "The door barely shuts behind her, and I hear, 'Hey, Jimbo! Catch!' and some kid tosses a couple cigarettes across the cafeteria. So this Jimbo character catches a cigarette in midair, but meantime the kids around him scramble and dive like they're going for a foul ball. Before I could even start yelling at them, these disgusting spit balls started whizzing by my head. So I start yelling, 'Hey—you there, with the red shirt'—cuz, 'course, I don't know their names yet—I say, 'Hey kid, you can't shoot spit balls in here!' And I mean, I didn't even get the words out of my mouth when these girls in the corner start screaming at each other."

"Whoa!" Olaf said. "What a zoo!"

"Wait! It gets worse!" I said, getting a little loud and worked up myself. "So the screaming girls—one of 'em, this redhead, goes, 'YOU GIVE ME THAT!' to another girl, who tosses this spiral notebook over her head like they're playing hot potato. Then Redhead grabs it, and they start this tug-of-war, with Redhead screeching, 'GIMME THAT SLAMBOOK!' I'm like, frozen, thinking, *What were those conflict resolution skills we learned in methods class*, and then I hear this Godawful *SCREEEEEEAACK!*"

"Oh no," Olaf said. "Holine . . . "

"Yeah. So, I look over at the other side of the room, tables screeching across the floor, books and pens flying sideways, and these two boys fall on top of each other, one just pummeling the other, so I start yelling, 'Boys! Boys!' Meanwhile, the other kids start screaming, 'FIGHT! FIGHT!' All the kids jump out of their seats, swarming like vultures to gawk at the ones just beating the hell out of each other."

"Oh my God, Holine," Olaf said, his eyes wide.

"Yeah," I said, gulping down some wine. "And so I push my way through, I grab the kid on top by the belt and I just start pulling like a madwoman. But I can't pull them apart: I lose my grip and fall backward, and next thing I know I'm on the floor, my stupid platform shoes flying out from under me."

"Get the hell out," he said, his mouth hanging open.

"And then—out of nowhere— there's this booming baritone behind me, 'WHAT IS GOING ON HERE?' and there's my master teacher looming over us, all six feet of her. Well, everyone just stopped cold. I kinda peeked up at her, then stood up and pulled my skirt back down over my tights. Talk about embarrassing."

"Oh man," Olaf said, but his lips quivered as he struggled to keep a straight face.

"Yeah, so she bellows, 'Children! This is our new student teacher's first day. Her *first* day! And this is how you welcome her? You all need to apologize this minute!' So, the kids say— you know, all together, in this kinda sing-song-y, mocking tone, 'Sorry, Miss Tee-cher.'"

Olaf burst into a fit of unrestrained laughter. I gave him a look, but suddenly I too dissolved into snorts of laughter. This got him going even more till we were both in hysterics, tears running down our faces.

"Wait . . . wait . . . you didn't even hear the best one," I laughed. "I get home, and I catch myself in the mirror, and I notice this little white pellet stuck in the side of my hair. I get the hand mirror to check the back, and there are more spit balls, just randomly stuck here and there like my hair's a damn Christmas tree, on my cardigan and one still stuck to my butt. So, all day— *all day*!—I walked around like that! Can you even imagine those kids laughing at my backside all day? A joke!" I said, cracking up all over again.

"But seriously, it's not just the kids. It's me," I said. "I don't think I'm cut out for this. You know me—I get tongue-tied and red-faced every time I'm in front of the class. Every day, I dread that drive to school, and all the way home, I ask myself, *What was I thinking?*" I stabbed a big chunk of lasagna, took a huge bite, but even the food in my mouth didn't stop me from venting. Still chewing, I managed to say, "And the papers! I spend every night grading papers. I'm too tired to go out any more, and I don't see any of my friends." I swallowed. "You know, I almost changed my major till Dad talked me out of it. 'Good career for a woman,'" he said. I took another gulp of wine.

"It helps to drink while you're reading the papers, too," he said, motioning to his wine. Then his face became serious. "Holine, think about it. You've only been at this for a month or so. And the kids you have—they're just *kids*, hardly out of grade school, trying to get attention, acting like big shots, just doing what they're supposed to do at this age."

"I know you're right. In my head, I know you're right," I said. "And I know it's my own fault for expecting—I don't know—something! *Meaningful* work. These kids don't care anything about what I'm teaching."

"Maybe not. But you're only seeing the ones who act out. The simple truth is this: you're never going to reach all of them," he said. "Believe me, none of us do. But think of the kid with the pocket protector, the kid that maybe is teased and bullied, hiding from the other kids how much he loves school. He could be me! I guarantee some of those quieter kids appreciate you already."

"I guess you're right," I said. "I have to keep trying. I feel a little better about it."

I actually did, and it wasn't the wine. It was Olaf, who had been my teacher before I ever set foot in a classroom.

The next day Olaf took me to the new Eastview Mall in Rochester so I could get my retail fix. The place was enormous, all gleaming steel and glass, shining chandeliers visible through floor to ceiling windows, sprawling department stores anchoring the corridors like mighty bookends. The mall parking lot was jammed with cars, and customers flooded the entrances from all directions. We had to park a good quarter mile from the doors, but, after the tangled traffic, we welcomed the walk, savoring the radiating sunshine, even warmer than the day before.

"Must be the great weather—look at all these . . . " I started, but was interrupted by Olaf's shriek of delight.

"ROSALINDA!" he cried, waving his little hand off, mischievous eyes searching ahead for "Rosalinda." For a split second, I was taken in myself, but then I remembered the game.

"Oh! Rosalinda! Rosalinda!" I cried out, and began waving like a madman, just like Olaf. Several people turned and looked—not at us, but ahead of us—for the illusory Rosalinda, who, they must've reasoned, was someone truly extraordinary. We kept it up, waving our hands wildly and looking far ahead, jumping up and down for effect. And, on cue, people from the parking lot started looking for Rosalinda too, actually craning their necks to see who could possibly have caused so much excitement.

We rushed into the mall, doubled over laughing, then speed-walked forward arm-in-arm, away from the people still looking far off, before anyone caught on that Rosalinda was only fictionally fabulous, our adult version of an imaginary friend. Other than the nose-bleed inducing platform sandals I bought— and which Olaf endorsed wholeheartedly, always encouraging my fanatical obsession with the most radical of shoes— it was the highlight of the afternoon. After a quick bite of pizza at Sbarro's, we made our way back to Olaf's to get ready for the play, which, as it turned out, wasn't a high school play at all.

A youth group from the local church had gotten permission to use the high school stage for their production of *Godspell.* Since there was one high school in town, the most talented kids joined in, church-goers or not. The church had paid one dollar in rent to make it legal.

How much worse could it get? I wondered to myself. But as the curtain rose, and a solitary voice began, "Prepare ye the way of the lord . . . " I was transfixed. The kid could really belt one out, and then the chorus joined in, blending into harmonies that were close to perfect. By the end of the song, which became more like a rock anthem as it rose to crescendo, the audience stood, clapping in unison. Olaf beamed at me, dancing in rhythm.

"I never say *I told you so,*" he laughed.

By the end of the play, both of us wiped tears from our eyes with the death scene dramatized through stark, propless staging, Jesus "chained" by ribbons tied to a makeshift fence behind him.

After the final bows, tie-dyed and breathless kids ran toward us, crying, "How'd we do? How'd we do? Did you like it?"

"*Like* it! You guys were terrific!" Olaf said. "What a performance! And your singing, *actual* music to my ears! All that practice paid off big time!"

A tiny girl, a flower wreath still adorning her flowing hair, came up behind us. She looked intently at Olaf, took both his hands in hers, and said, "Thank you for running my lines with me. I wouldn't have remembered a word without your help. When I saw you in the audience, I pretended I was singing my lines to you, just like rehearsal."

"Darcy," Olaf started, giving her a fatherly nod and wink, "See? I told you that you had it in you! You were amazing!"

The lead, an afro-headed twig of a kid still in his Superman shirt and suspenders, came by too, and deadpanned, "Far out, man. You came." Then he reached out his hand to shake Olaf's.

Just then, a man came up behind us, and extending his hand to Olaf said, "My God! Are you the teacher Anthony can't stop talking about? My kid loves your class—wait . . . ah . . . Helen! Helen! Come meet Anthony's teacher." It wasn't long before a group of students and parents encircled Olaf, who congratulated and praised, commended and complimented one after another till he finally made his way toward the door.

On the way home, Olaf and I couldn't stop talking about the play—the set design, the talent, the energy, the heart. The kids had given it their all.

"You know what struck me the most?" I asked him.

"The Jesus kid, right? Anthony—he's astonishing," Olaf beamed. "Such a sensitive reading for a seventeen-year-old."

"Yeah, he was great," I said. "But what impressed me the most is how much they love you. You'd have thought Jesus himself had come to congratulate them. I don't know how you do it."

"I just try to be myself. I pretty much ignore everything we learned in those education classes—you know, reinforce learning by blah, blah, blah," Olaf glanced over at me, nodding encouragingly, and continued, "When you're truly yourself, people appreciate that. When you get all that crap out of your head—the stuff about what you're supposed to do—and let your hair down a little, be the Holine that I know, I guarantee your students will come around too."

"I hope you're right," I answered, "but I can never be you. You're a damn kid magnet."

"We might do it a little differently," he said. "You know me—I reel 'em in by acting goofy. I jump around, exaggerate like a cartoon till their laughing at me becomes, well, just laughing. In no time you'll be even better at it than I am." He hesitated, and taking on a more earnest tone, continued, "Seriously, Holine. You have a certain kind of strength; a natural leader is hiding under those shy eyes. I know it as sure as I know you. When you get out of your head a little, you're going to find it. And then everyone else will see it too."

"Thanks, Olaf," I said. "But you might be just a tad prejudiced."

"Just take it day-by-day," he said. "Day-by-day . . . get it?" And, with typical gusto and goofy joy, he burst into the famous song from *Godspell.* I couldn't help singing along.

I hoped the song would still be ringing in my head when the morning bell rang again at Kennedy Middle School.

But it would not be as much fun, singing it alone.

Chapter Seven
1977

I walked among the angry and sad gay sisters and brothers last night at City Hall and late last night as they lit candles and stood in silence on Castro Street reaching out for some symbolic thing that would give them hope . . . And YOU have to give them hope. Hope for better world. Hope for a better tomorrow . . . Hope that all will be alright.

—Harvey Milk, San Francisco Gay Community Center, *Harvey Milk: An Archive of Hope*

"Holine! Holine!" I heard Olaf before I saw him. "Over here!" I turned toward Seventh, and there he was, running toward me, his black shoes squeaking newness.

Just moments before, I'd stood in front of Carnegie Hall, looking east on 57th, then west, then east again—that is, when I wasn't taking in the live theater of the city itself: cars and yellow cabs winding in and out of lanes, horns blaring; chatty concert-goers in crisp tuxedos and sequined gowns intermixed with gawking tourists, Nikons hanging from straps around their necks; real New Yorkers in business suits casting disdainful glances at the interlopers while expertly gliding through and around the crowds, their years of experience enabling an uncanny sense of pedestrian rhythm.

I walked one way, then the other, under the hall's five black canopies, each bordered with a line of subtle, tasteful lights—so unlike the flashing frenzy of Times Square just blocks away. Each canopy hung from one of five enormous arched windows. The canopies, meant to protect well-heeled concert-goers from weather, weren't needed on that glorious spring evening. The sun was just setting on the city, basked in twilight. On each of the stately brownstone pillars was a sign encased in glass, the hall's refined equivalent of a marquee. *Chicago Symphony Orchestra, Beethoven's Missa Solemnis, Sir Georg Solti, Conductor, 8 PM,* the sign read. Underneath was a quote attributed to the maestro, the renowned conductor who'd dazzled audiences in Munich, Vienna, London, but called his affiliation with the Chicago Symphony "the greatest musical love relationship of my life."

Every minute or so, the reality of where I found myself—and why—rushed back: I was in front of Carnegie Hall, waiting for Olaf. I still couldn't fully grasp all that had happened. In one short year, Olaf had quit his teaching job, moved to Illinois, entered a graduate program in vocal music, auditioned for the Chicago Symphony Chorus and was accepted. And I was actually here, in my Caché black halter dress, its hem barely grazing the top of my four-inch strappy sandals. My chestnut hair—halfway to my waist, ends clipped to an even, blunt line—hung straight and heavy over my dress, revealing only an occasional glimpse of my exposed back. I was shiny; I was 22-years-old. Every so often, I realized a stare and whispers from passing tourists meant they thought I might *be* somebody. And for a moment, I thought maybe I was somebody. Any place else I was content to fade into the wallpaper. But in New York, everything was new—even me. And now, in the midst of my fantasy come-to-life, there was Olaf.

"Oh, my Olaf!" I said, and rushed into his arms. He extended his arms to look at me; his eyes flashed with excitement. "Isn't this just so cool?" I said, and then, backing up to get a better look at him, "Wow! I haven't seen you in a tux in forever—probably—I don't know—senior ball. You look amazing!" Trim and slender in his classic black tuxedo, starched white shirt, neatly tied bow at the neck, Olaf was a veritable Carnegie Hall poster.

"Our uniform," he said, smiling modestly. "And, you too! What a dress!" he said, and then, looking around, "Where's Mom and Dad?"

"Waiting in the vestibule," I said. "C'mon! Let's go find them."

"OK—I only have a couple minutes," he said. "Then it's—backstage!"

After Olaf gave Mom and Dad a quick hug and kiss, he dashed away, and we found our seats in the orchestra. We settled into the plush red velvet cushions, then gazed up and behind us like the shameless tourists we were, unable to resist the urge to take it all in. I had never seen such a place. A half-circle of several rows—a sweeping parterre, mezzanine, balcony, each row trimmed in tasteful eggshell and rimmed with lights, like an elaborate, multi-layered wedding cake—rose above and behind us in majestic grace. Over our heads, an embedded circular panel delicately lit the hall, casting a halo of subtle beams on the stage and the audience. Though I held a linen-fiber program in my hand, its words raised like Braille and embossed in gold, I was so enamored with the spectacle, I couldn't even search for Olaf's name just yet. And the concert hadn't even begun.

The lights dimmed. Lines of tuxedo-clad musicians cradled flutes, violins, and oboes as they marched in lock-step to their seats on stage. On our right—actually stage left—the members of the chorus paraded from the wings, silently filling in the risers.

"There he is!" I whispered to my mother, squeezing her arm.

"Oh! I see him," she began, excited as if she hadn't just seen him minutes before. "Honey! Look—there he is!" she said to Dad, who also seemed stunned that Olaf was actually there.

Suddenly the audience rose in unison, emitting a roar of applause and appreciative shouts, as Sir Georg Solti entered from stage right, bowed gracefully, and then took his place on a platform, front and center. At his appearance, an oboe held a solitary note. Seconds later, violins, flutes, viola, and horns chimed in, tuning to the exact tone of the first-chair oboe. Then the orchestra's seamless unison dissolved into a cacophony of scales and trills. The maestro nodded firmly, drawing his arms wide and slowly drawing his fingers together, gesturing for quiet—the silence sudden, as though he'd turned a switch. On cue, the audience calmed to a hush. The maestro whispered intimately to his beloved orchestra as we waited in solemn silence. Then he raised his baton.

Soaring strings and thundering tympanies expanded in an upsurge of harmonic grandeur. The effect on me was unlike my response to any music I'd ever heard; it was an actual, physical sensation, chords rising up through my chest and ending at my eyes, wet with fresh tears. The chorus joined in a resonant undercurrent, separate, distinct tenors, baritones, altos and sopranos, blending into the harmonic euphoria of the Kyrie. It was the sound of heaven. Within the magical, swelling strains, I heard my brother's voice. I knew it as I knew my own, as if inside my own head. From my seat in the darkened theater, I could barely make out Dad's face. Even in the half-light, I spied a silent tear trickling down his cheek.

The maestro was a show unto himself, engaged in a feat of intense physical exertion, somehow merging athleticism with art. He waved his baton with furious energy, his arms jerking upward vigorously, generating rhythms ranging from powerfully turbulent to somber and serene. He bent and beckoned, his body language extracting the blend of sounds exactly as he willed them to unfold. He played the orchestra as if it was a singular instrument, coaxing and hushing here, releasing a fury there. Every so often, he'd swish his left hand over his bald dome, as if brushing away imaginary hair. If the music was our rapture, the maestro was the show.

After the concert, Mom, Dad and I followed the crowd onto the wide sidewalk, bathed in the glare of streetlights and colorful storefront signs. We walked toward our planned meeting place and waited at the corner. Mom and Dad couldn't stop gushing about the concert—the sights and sounds and the very miracle of Olaf at Carnegie Hall. I looked up to see Olaf coming around the side of the building with three other tuxedo-clad guys, two of whom held hands. As I raised my hand so he could find us in the crowd, he said something I couldn't hear to the hand-holders, who dropped hands and followed him toward us. Mom had seen me motion to them. I wasn't sure if she'd seen anything else.

"Hey guys! Did you enjoy it?" Olaf asked happily, grabbing Mom and giving her a kiss on the cheek.

"It was marvelous . . . just marvelous!" Dad said. "Unbelievable! Well done!"

"Thanks, Dad," Olaf said. "And hey, I'd like you to meet my fellow tenors, John, Andres and Sal."

"Happy to meet you," Dad said, "and to congratulate you. What a performance!" Dad extended his hand, and shook with one guy, then the next two.

"And this is my mom, and my sister, Jennifer," Olaf said. "Well, I call her 'Holine.'"

I watched for a sign that Mom had seen Olaf's hand-holding friends, and there it was. Rigid lines formed on her face.

She smiled weakly through gritted teeth and extended a limp hand, shaking politely with John, then Andres, then Sal, but with obvious restraint. I wondered if they noticed or if I just knew her too well. And Dad, well . . . he either didn't notice or pretended not to.

"Hello. Good to meet you," she said stiffly. Then nothing.

"Oh my God!" I said, trying to salvage their impression of us. "You all were amazing! I have never heard such sweet sounds, like angels!"

"Thanks—Holine, is it?" Andres said, shaking my hand warmly.

"Yup—the silly names we call each other!' I said. "You can call me Holine or any other name you want. As long as you keep inviting me to your concerts."

"Guys, we're heading out for a couple drinks to celebrate," Olaf said. "Meet you back at Aunt Ruthie's. I won't be too late." Then, misreading Mom's anxious eyes, he said, "Stop worrying! I can read a subway map."

"Have fun, guys," Dad said. Olaf and his friends turned and walked in the direction of Times Square. Dad stepped off the curb and raised his arm, hailing a taxi.

When Mom, Dad and I got to Aunt Ruthie's, I went right to bed, the music in my head lulling me into the deepest sleep I'd had in weeks—none of my usual stewing about my stalled job search or any of the countless worries—real and imagined—that usually kept me spinning half the night. Instead, I remained restful under the soothing spell of Georg Solti's musical genius, the grandeur of Carnegie Hall, and the noisy, beautiful mess that is New York City. That is, until seven the next morning, when I awoke with a start.

"Gizzy! Gizzy!" Aunt Ruthie scolded her yipping poodle, Gizmo. "Gizzy, quiet down! We have guests! Gizzy! Come here this minute! Mama has a treat for you!"

It took me a moment, but then I remembered: We were in New York—well, almost . . . if you counted Queens. I looked at the clock: 7:03. If I got right up and got Olaf moving, we'd have the day to wander the streets. I threw back the covers, rummaged through my suitcase for toiletries, my shower cap, my favorite outfit and headed into the bathroom to shower.

As I walked downstairs, the aroma of percolating coffee and freshly-cooked bacon wafted up from the kitchen. Mom, Dad and Olaf were already up and sitting around the breakfast table. Aunt Ruthie, who scrambled from stove to electric coffee pot to the table, simultaneously cooked bacon, flipped pancakes, poured coffee and filled Gizmo's tiny dish with cooled bacon that she'd cut into tiny squares. On the table were cups and saucers, cream and sugar, an oversized bowl of oranges and bananas, a plateful of walnuts with a nutcracker laid across them, a bottle of Aunt Jemima syrup, a platter of croissants, a pitcher of orange juice, a liter of generic diet soda, and three boxes of Entenmann's pastries.

"Well, here is the princess now," Aunt Ruthie said. I thought I detected a trace of sarcasm in her voice, but I couldn't be sure. "Already in her make-up and ready to go. Don't you want to tie your hair back while you have breakfast?" she asked.

"Thanks, Aunt Ruthie, but I'm not big on breakfast," I said. "Just coffee will be fine."

"Nonsense!" she said. "Here, pour yourself some juice, and try a croissant. And some Entenmann's—you have to try the Entenmann's," she insisted. I poured some juice. Olaf, his hair sticking up on one side, grinned at me, rolling his eyes when Aunt Ruthie turned back toward bacon sizzling on the stove, her oversized Hawaiian muumuu billowing and swaying over plump little legs. Aunt Ruthie always wore stockings, but for some reason that I couldn't understand, she would roll them down to her ankles where they ended, tied in a tight circle like little sausages. She chatted incessantly, stopping only to chastise Gizzy, who snatched her bacon bits, carried them one-by-one into the living room and dropped them on the white shag carpet, dribbling greasy crumbs as she chewed. "Gizzy!" she cried, oil dripping from her spatula as she turned toward the tiny bandit. "Bad dog! Why, you little . . . " she started, then burst into howls of laughter as the dog gobbled up the remaining bacon before it could be snatched away.

Without asking, Aunt Ruthie heaped several pancakes on Mom's plate. "Have some juice—or would you rather have tomato? I have tomato. Or apple?" and reaching into the refrigerator with her unspatula-ed hand, she produced bottles of various juices.

"Ruthie, Ruthie! There's enough food for an army!" Mom said. "C'mon, sit with us. We haven't seen a spread like this since there were ten of us kids around Mom's table."

"Look at all this! You *must* have some more pancakes and bacon," Aunt Ruthie insisted, serving Olaf before he could refuse, then stepping behind his chair and giving him an affectionate squeeze. "My handsome nephew!" she fawned over him, as she always did. "Here. Have an orange. They're very good." She poured herself a heaping glass of diet ginger ale and finally collapsed in a chair across from me, pulling Gizmo onto her lap.

Smiling broadly at Mom, she said, "We *have* to shop on the Steinway today. The stores are fabulous! Nothing like you have at home." Aunt Ruthie took a big bite of her pastry, washing it down with ginger ale.

"I'd love that," Mom said. "You kids coming, or what are your plans?"

Ugh, I thought. Steinway Street was the main shopping thoroughfare in Astoria—not my idea of a stimulating experience, visiting who-knows-how-many old lady stores. I ached for real New York.

"We'd like to," Olaf said, "Really . . . if only there was more time, but we wanted to go to the Village, then see if we can nab tickets for *Pippin.* You know . . . before it closes."

"Oh, I'd stay away from the Village," Aunt Ruthie said. "You really gotta watch yourself there. Hooligans everywhere doing God-knows-what. You're better off staying around here. Never had trouble on the Steinway."

"I think they can handle themselves," Dad said. "Besides, I should think you girls want some sister time, right? We can meet the kids for dinner. Rockefeller Center, 5:30? That'll give you time to get to the show." I cast a thankful glance in his direction. Between the coffee and the conversation, I couldn't stop my foot from shaking and my fingers drumming the table.

"I'm gonna hit the shower," Olaf said.

"I'll come up too," I said and followed Olaf, both of us giggling as we tripped up the stairs, thankful that, with Dad's help, our escape was in the bag. When I came back down, jacket already on, I busied myself by tracing our proposed route on a subway map. Minutes later, Olaf rushed down the stairs wearing a military-style hat with red piping and a vest to match—his "uniform" for his part-time job as a singing telegram delivery man. He marched into the kitchen and, to the tune of "You're A Grand Old Flag," sang at the top of his voice, "You're a grand old aunt, you're a fast-cooking aunt, and forever in sweets may you reign! You're the emblem of the aunt I love, we eat here with glee, you're my fave!"

Mom and Dad cracked up, Aunt Ruthie howled with laughter, and Gizmo yelped and yipped. I just sat there, shaking my head.

An hour later, I followed Olaf up a flight of grimy stairs littered with cigarette butts and ancient chewing gum pounded gray into the concrete by countless footsteps. I felt the sun before I got to the top, inhaled the ever-present exhaust and the steamed hot dog scent of street vendors. Getting our bearings, we realized our location, Varick and Houston. I could easily navigate upper Manhattan with its numbered streets and avenues, but here in the Village, I was lost. I assumed my New York mask of indifference—Olaf had taught me that—and followed him toward Bleecker, then Christopher and back to Carmine. We fake-scowled our way, maneuvering in and around the crowds.

We took in the sights surreptitiously, sneaking glances at the queens dressed in over-the-top street drag; the block script graffiti—*RAMONES*—in fierce red lettering painted on the side of a crumbling building; a crane looming over Sixth Avenue that moved ancient pieces of city, one huge cinderblock at a time. A city bus gasped to a stop, releasing weary workers, their dark, hooded heads bobbing as they descended the stairs, hit the street and vanished into the crowd.

In front of the red brick Stonewall Inn, a lone trumpeter wailed a melancholy *Moon River*, random coins in a pail nestled between his feet. Taxis blasted their horns as they weaved in and out in their daily game of chicken, snaking around the buses and barely beating the mob of pedestrians that crossed as the light flashed green. Smashed paper cups, dented beer cans, plastic wrappers and syringes clustered along the edge of grates beside the curb. We walked straight down Carmine toward throngs of people about our age—mostly NYU students—who waited in line outside Joe's Pizza.

"Whoa! Pizza!" Olaf said, heading toward the shop, to which he seemed magnetically drawn. He breathed in the spicy, doughy smell. "C'mon, Holine."

"I'm in," I said. We waited in line, then grabbed two slices, so large their points hung off the edge of flimsy white paper plates. Kids sat side-by-side at the counter on stools leaking stuffing through old, cracked vinyl, every seat in the closet-sized shop taken. We crossed the street to Father Demo Square, a half-block, triangular park surrounded by sprawling bushes, the bright green of early spring. Olaf led the way to an empty bench.

Two benches away, a man in drag sat alone. He smiled shyly in our direction, revealing a mouthful of rotted teeth, then rose, scattering crumbs and bits of pizza crust across the lawn to the delight of swarming pigeons. Then he turned toward Carmine Street and walked off, the hem of his skirt grayed and fraying, beaten by the street. Olaf sighed sadly.

"Too many people have no one," he said. "Even here, where people are everywhere."

"Yeah," I said. "I guess you can be surrounded by people and still be lonely."

"It's tough, finding your place in all this," he said, shaking his head. Remembering his pizza, he took a bite, pulling at the still-hot, stringy cheese.

"And Chicago?" I asked. "Is it the same there?"

"Not for me," he said. "I have Teddy. And I'm in a fine arts program, for God's sake! I have never felt so accepted, never been surrounded by people like me. We're like family. Family that got to choose each other, even."

"It does my heart good to hear that," I said, throwing my left arm around his shoulder. "And Andres and Sal—they seem like good people."

"Oh, yeah—we're together so much—rehearsals, recordings, performances. We've gotten totally close."

"So, you all had fun last night?" I asked.

"*Great* time," he said. "That performance! Something that special, well, we just didn't want the night to end. We couldn't stop talking about it, just reliving every note."

"I know," I said. "Even for me. And I was only in the audience. I know I'll never forget it."

"And Miss Hillis—she was ecstatic! Hugged and kissed every one of us when it was over." Margaret Hillis was the Choral Director, something I'd never have known if I hadn't heard it over and over again from Olaf: "Miss Hillis this, Miss Hillis that." Olaf had mentioned her constantly during our phone conversations over the past year. He adored her mothering, her discipline, her devotion. The matriarch of the choral family.

"Did you catch Mom's reaction?" I asked. "You know, to your friends?"

"I did," Olaf said. He shrugged. "Guess I should be used to it by now."

"Yeah," I said. "Kinda like high school all over again?"

"Oh, you don't know the half of it," he said.

"Yeah—what happened, anyway?"

"The stuff we went through—me and Mom," he said. "I try not to think about it."

"That bad?"

"Especially that last year," Olaf said. "It all started when she found some notes."

"Notes?" I asked.

"Notes I wrote Chris—remember him?" he asked.

"Yeah, vaguely."

"Yeah, well—notes from me to him, from him back to me . . ." he began. "The notes made clear . . . let's just say, we weren't merely friends," he said, casting his eyes downward at the memory.

"Oh God. That must've been a scene."

"But that's not all," he said. "I actually came out to her—before the notes."

"You *told* her?"

"I did," he said. "I don't know. I thought just maybe she'd . . . well, if not accept it, just understand. *Something*," he looked down at his half-eaten pizza. "Boy. Was I wrong."

"What'd she do?" I asked.

"She dismissed it—said it was some kinda phase. She said it, you know, too sweetly, like I was just a dumb, silly kid. 'Oh, you're just mixed up. You just have a little crush on a friend. You'll see. Before long you'll find a girl.'"

"Oh dear God." I had to look in his eyes to make sure he was serious. His eyes were just sad.

"Yeah, and when I insisted that no, it wasn't a boy-crush thing," he said, "or whatever she called it . . . she did something I just . . . well, to this day, it's hard to forgive."

"Oh no," I said, afraid of what he might say next. "What, what do you mean?"

"She starts snooping around and finds the notes," he said. "Then a week later, she drags me to the doctor—this old quack she'd gone to for like a hundred years. So he could *fix* me." He shook his head and covered his face with his hands.

"Noooooo!" I said. "Not that guy that gave us our polio shot when we were, like, five?"

"That's the one," he said. "*So* humiliating."

"Oh, honey," I said. "I'm so sorry."

"Oh, there's more," he said. "I had to have a physical and answer a bunch of embarrassing questions. Then the jerk met with her privately, didn't even *talk* to me. He gave her some psychobabble—something like I was too close to her and not close enough to Dad. 'A classic case of confused sexual identity,' he said. Basically, he told her I was confused because I was in love with her." Olaf picked randomly at pizza crumbs, flicking them onto the grass where a cluster of pigeons swooped down, pecking madly at the morsels.

"You can't be serious," I took his hand. "Oh my God, Olaf."

"I'm afraid so," he said, sadly. "But you know what's even sicker? It was *how* she said it. She was so relieved—she had the explanation she wanted." He hesitated, swallowing hard, blinking back a tear. When he regained his composure, he said, "Naturally, that's when I stopped talking to her about it." He was quiet for a moment. Sipping the last of his Coke, he stared at the pigeons who suddenly flew upward in a singular, communal motion, and perched on the eaves of a nearby building. "In some ways, you almost can't blame her. I mean, part of it was saving her own face—I get that. And when I think of how she grew up, so sheltered."

"I know, but . . ."

"I have to believe she just didn't want me to struggle," he said. "It would be a harder life. She was right about that."

"I just—I'm so sorry," I said. "I wish I'd been the older one. At least you would have had someone to talk to."

"It's OK," he said. "I do now."

He squeezed my hand, and we sat quietly, two newly-minted New Yorkers in our little West Village oasis.

The next morning, I woke again to the smell of coffee and bacon and pastries and syrup, but this time, I shuffled down in my robe and slippers. Olaf was already at the table.

"Morning, Aunt Ruthie. Morning, O." I said. "I'm still singing *Pippin* songs in my head. I was dreaming them! Aunt Ruthie! We got to see Ben Vereen. *Ben Vereen!* He was so good . . ."

Olaf interrupted, "I was just on my way out. C'mon, Holine," he said. "Come with me. Hurry, put some clothes on."

"What?" I yawned. "C'mon where?"

"With me!" he said, more urgently. "To the newsstand."

"What are you talking about?" I asked.

"To get the *Times!* The *Times* review of Carnegie Hall!" he said, like I should have known why he desperately needed the paper. "Let's *go!*"

"But, your breakfast!" Aunt Ruthie said.

"Back in a flash, Auntie," Olaf said, and turning to me, "Just go throw something on. Hurry!"

"I'm a wreck," I said, rubbing the sleep from my eyes. "I haven't even put a brush through my hair."

"Do I look like I'm taking 'no' for an answer?" He pulled out my chair. "C'mon."

"Oh, all right," I said, and started back up the stairs. "At least pour me some coffee?"

I threw on some jeans and put a scarf on my head to cover my rat's nest of hair. When I got back downstairs, Olaf was already standing in the doorway, without my coffee.

As soon as we were out the door, he started jogging. I followed, unable to keep up, still trying to shake off the morning fog. The newsstand was only two blocks away, and when it was fully in sight, Olaf broke into a full sprint. By the time I reached him, he'd already paid for the paper and was frantically turning pages.

"Here . . . here it is. Let's see. "Blah, blah, blah . . . symphony 'unusually austere in tone and primarily oriented toward the classic symphonic repertory . . . drama aplenty in the carefully judged dynamic accents, the lithe tensile motion and the finely graded tempo transitions . . . " He stopped a moment, then his eyes brightened, widened with joy and celebration, as he read ever faster and louder. "'There could be no complaint about the technical execution, particularly from Margaret Hillis's superbly trained chorus, which sang with a precision of pitch, tone, and dynamic control that was altogether breathtaking!' *Breathtaking*, Holine! *The New York Times*!"

I snatched the paper out of his hands. "Let me see that!"

I read it to myself, and he said, "Read it, read it again!" So I read aloud and added the sentence that followed. "'The orchestra, too, never made a false step—the instrumental blend was unfailingly lustrous and perfectly balanced.' Olaf! Raves! From *The New York Times*. Wait till Dad hears this!" I could not contain myself, both of us jumping up and down, hugging, jumping up and down some more.

We ran back to tell Mom, Dad, and Aunt Ruthie, who were sitting at the breakfast table, Mom and Dad already dressed for the airport, their tidy suitcases packed and waiting beside the door. Practically plowing into them and totally out of breath from running all the way back to the house, Olaf started excitedly, "The *Times* review . . . it's so good . . . breathtaking . . . they said we were breathtaking." He held his side a minute, and I finished his sentence, then he finished mine, both of us adding to the story, taking turns reading and rereading one quote, then another, and then shoving the papers in their faces just to make sure they believed us. Mom, Dad and Aunt Ruthie looked startled, then crazy with joy. They laughed, they clapped, they took turns reading for themselves. Finally, we sat down, took a breath, and began to laugh hysterically. Aunt Ruthie found some champagne in her cabinet, and poured five glasses. We toasted my darling Olaf, the Chicago Symphony, Miss Hillis, *The New York Times*, and the city itself.

And we reread that article so many times, we didn't realize the time.

"Oh, my God!" Olaf said. "We gotta get packing. My flight's in three hours! C'mon, Holine." He and I sprinted up the stairs and haphazardly tossed shirts and shoes and toiletries in our bags. In moments, we were on the street, Dad's arm upraised to hail a taxi. He whistled loudly, having seen too many movies where a whistle miraculously conjures a cab on cue. And in line with the good fortune that had followed us all morning, a yellow cab squealed around the corner, stopping just beyond the curb.

We'd barely gotten through security at La Guardia when Olaf's flight to Chicago was called.

"Bye! I love you all!" Olaf said, embracing Mom so fiercely, he lifted her off the ground. "Thank you for coming! I'll never forget it." He gave Dad a bear hug, then turned to me. "Holine. *Magical* time. Love you!" Tears of joy mingled with my usual heartbreak at leaving him.

"We'll always have this weekend," I said. At that, he dashed into the tunnel toward his plane.

I moved over to the wall-wide windows and watched as, even from this distance, I could see the movement of tiny heads through the plane's many portholes. I thought I spotted Olaf, but I couldn't be sure. The engine began to grind, revving up to a steady whine.

"C'mon, Jen," Dad whispered, taking my arm. "It's worse to watch."

We walked off together toward our gate, but I couldn't help looking back as the plane began its ascent, lifting higher and higher, finally obscured by clouds.

I hadn't thought about Carnegie Hall for a while, when, months later, I was back home, living with Mom and Dad, substituting at the local high school by day and applying for teaching jobs in the evening.

One February night after combing through the *TV Guide*, I started in on Dad.

"C'mon, Dad," I pleaded. "It's the Grammy Awards!"

"Awards?" he teased. "For that noise you call *music*?" Despite his protest, he reluctantly changed the channel, then retreated behind his newspaper. After a syrupy performance by Debbie Boone, even I began to zone out. When a running list of the Grammys for classical recordings awarded earlier in the day lit up the screen, my eyes began to glaze over. I was just about to head up to bed. Then, I saw it.

"DAD!" I screamed. "Solti!—Dad! Dad! The Chicago Symphony! Margaret Hillis! Dad! He *won!* Olaf!—he *won!*"

Mom came screaming down the stairs to see what was all the fuss. Dad sat up with a jolt, just in time to see it in print before the next award took its place on the screen.

I jumped to my feet. "Mom! A *Grammy*! Olaf won a Grammy!" I swung her around in a wild dance, the two of us spinning and circling around the den. "Quick! We gotta call him!" I grabbed for the phone and dialed the number without looking, my muscle memory kicking in. I waited.

"It's ringing!" I said, my hand over the mouthpiece. I waited, tensed in anticipation. The phone rang and rang. Finally after one too many rings, I hung up. My shoulders sank.

"Oh well," Mom said. "We can try again tomorrow."

"K," I said. But I couldn't help myself. I dialed again. The phone rang, rang, rang. No answer.
No Olaf.

Chapter Eight
1981

In the period October 1980-May 1981, 5 young men, all active homosexuals, were treated for biopsy-confirmed Pneumocystis carinii pneumonia at 3 different hospitals in Los Angeles, California. Two of the patients died. All 5 patients had laboratory-confirmed previous or current cytomegalovirus (CMV) infection and candida mucosal infection.

—Morbidity and Mortality Weekly Report

I sat at a wobbly wooden desk facing the class in our half of the cafeteria, checking names on my roster while trying to repress my uniquely dreadful nausea, an acidic queasiness that lodged deep in my throat and stuck there, that I could neither swallow or throw up. Kids filtered in. In a matter of minutes, they filled the seats in front of me, some of them sleepwalking; others rushing toward their friends to share gossip, notes, gum, pens and pencils; still others scrambling to copy another kid's homework. The steady hum of voices rose, chairs squeaking as kids clustered closer together. Another kid scraped a chair into the corner, slammed his head down on the desk, and shut his eyes, dreaming himself elsewhere. I could relate.

By third period, my queasiness had subsided and, after dashing to the bathroom between classes, I arrived, breathless, and stood in front of my class of tenth-graders, my favorite class of the day.

"Mz. B," Nate said, taking his seat in the front row. "No quiz today, right?"

"What's that?" I teased. "You say you want a quiz?"

"No—pleeeeeeze! No quiz," he pleaded. "We had extra-long practice last night . . . "

"Practice?" I asked. "C'mon, Nate. You know how well that excuse works on me."

"Aw, please, Mz. B.," he said. "I read *most* of it."

"Yeah," Laura chimed in from her seat next to him. Every day was a race to see which of them could sit closest to my desk. "This book is *jive*. I don't get half those crazy words. How'm I sposed to understand what he's talking about?" She waved her dog-eared copy of *A Tale of Two Cities* in the air.

"You have a dictionary at home?" I asked. Laura shrugged.

"So, let's do this," I said. "Stop sign. You guys ever done that?"

"Stop sign?" Laura asked.

"You'll see. Hmmm . . . four chapters . . . thirty pages. So let's get in groups of three. Each group takes three pages. One person gets a dictionary from the shelf and is the word-finder, one takes notes, one reads aloud. Each time anyone in the group comes to a word that he or she doesn't understand, that person puts a hand forward—you know, like a signal to stop." I demonstrated. "Then together, you try to guess at what it might mean, given how it's used. The person with the dictionary looks up the word to see how close you came." I made a chart on the board to illustrate.

"Not *groupwork*," students groaned in unison. "*Awww*, come on Mz. B.!" they continued, even while they dutifully slid desks together.

"OK, guys," I said. "I'll go first, so you get the idea. I'll read, and you make the stop sign when I come to a word you don't know." I began to read. "'It was the best of times, it was the worst of times.'" I got as far as the second line and the word, "epoch," when several hands signaled me to stop. "OK, *epoch*. Listen again to the beginning of that sentence: ' . . . it was the age of wisdom, it was the age of foolishness, it was the epoch of belief.' What do the words before 'epoch' suggest it might mean?"

"Epoch?" Josh asked. "I thought it said *epic*. You know, like you go to the Petty concert, and you're telling your friends, you know, that riff was *epic*, man. Like the riff in *Refugee*." Josh played air guitar and sang the for effect, "We got something, we both know it . . . "

"OK, getting my fishing pole to reel you back in," I said, motioning as if hooking Josh on the end of imaginary fishing line and winding the reel on my make-believe pole. "Tom Petty. Yes, his performance could be considered 'epic.' But *epic* is an altogether different word that means something is especially significant, on a grand scale . . . legendary."

"Legendary!" Josh cried. "Yeah, that's it!"

"Does anyone know how to spell 'epic'?" I asked.

Voices from around the room chanted in unison, "e...p...i...c" as I wrote it on the board.

"Laura, you have a dictionary," I said. "Now, would you find 'epoch' and read us the definition?" Laura searched the pages, then read, "The beginning of a new and important period." "Yes, so notice, class: in this instance, 'epoch' is a synonym for "age" or "season," words Dickens uses right before switching to 'epoch.' Now imagine if he hadn't switched and just kept using 'age' or 'season.'"

"That would be boring as hell to read," Nate said.

"Exactly," I said. "He was being inventive! Now, do you also see how you can use the sentences around the word you don't know to figure out a meaning?" A few heads nodded. "So, now your turn. Go!"

I smiled to myself as I circulated among the students, offering clues and answering questions, I realized they were having fun in spite of themselves. By the end of the period, we had a list of words—*epoch, incredulity, superlative, prophetic*—words that the students were unlikely to forget.

Later that day, I sat alone in the parking lot outside the school board office, my maternity leave paperwork in a manilla folder on the seat beside me. Derek, the "tough" guy; Josh, the music-lover; Nate, the athlete; Laura, the nonconformist. I couldn't help worrying about them and what would happen to them while I was home on maternity leave. But, no—that wasn't it at all. What would happen to *me* without *them*—that was what caused me to sit in my car for a full half hour before I picked up the folder and walked into the office.

I'd worked so hard to become a teacher, my conversations with Olaf about lessons and methods as numerous as the students I'd encountered. Now, three years after my wedding to Paul and three years of teaching behind me, I'd be a mom instead—something I had no clue how to be.

In June, I screwed pieces of the crib together, setting it against the pale yellow wall and arranging the fluffy tea-rose bumper around the sides. I placed the only stuffed animal I'd bought—a fluffy, vanilla-colored Teddy bear—in the center. I folded tiny onesies and footed pajamas; I lined up Pampers and soft knitted booties on the shelf under the changing table. With my due date approaching in those last days of summer, I dreamed my baby, actually saw his pink cheeks, his full head of dark hair. So, when he was born two weeks early, on a late

August day, I recognized him: Paul Joseph II—someone I already knew and loved—and all my worries dissipated with the languishing summer days. Life would begin again, through my son. He was healthy and strong, right from the beginning, lifting his little head as if to check out his new surroundings.

Visitors clustered around the nursery window, eager for a peek. Mom wanted more—she could hardly contain herself, holding and kissing the baby before the nurses had a chance to intervene; Dad smiled proudly from the sidelines, his eyes full, almost disbelieving he actually had a grandson. In-laws, aunts, cousins and friends came to bid their fond wishes and leave blue-trimmed packages full of blankets, bibs, and board books.

The only one missing was Olaf, away on his first trip to Italy. I'd have to wait a few weeks to introduce him to his nephew.

When Olaf finally arrived at my house a few weeks later, he surprised me, sneaking up the steps toward the nursery as I stood, my back to the door, gently rocking the baby back-and-forth, staring out the window at the orange-tipped maples. I kissed the top of the baby's tiny head, relishing the tuft of fine, downy hair that grazed my cheek, breathing in his powder soft smell. His swaddled warmth, his full weight against my chest was worth the pain radiating up my spine from holding him too long. I couldn't bring myself to peel him away and put him down just yet.

I felt someone watching us, then glanced up to see Olaf in the doorway. He took in the scene as if wishing to freeze the moment.

"Oh, Holine!" Olaf whispered. "What a beautiful boy!"

"Olaf!" I whispered, careful not to disturb the baby in my arms. "You're here! Finally!" I stooped over the baby and gave Olaf a peck on the cheek.

"My God, Holine. That face! What a perfect little dumpling! He's . . . wow! He's big Paul!"

"That's what everyone says," I smiled, adding softly, "Wait till you see the baby pictures, Paul's and the baby's, side-by-side. Clones, for God's sake."

I gently lay the baby in his cradle and covered him with a pastel blanket decorated with tiny yellow ducklings. We stood over Paul Joe, Olaf and I, just taking in the moment, both of us transfixed by the peaceful in-and-out of his tiny baby breaths.

"That precious face," whispered Olaf as we tiptoed downstairs to the kitchen. "He's beautiful, miraculous! And already playing tricks on his uncle, arriving early like that, when I'm not even back home yet!"

"Yeah, well what was worse for you was sure better for me," I said. "The summer was brutal. Remind me to time my pregnancies better next time."

"You should've seen me . . . pacing around the airport, on stand-by, checking the board, pestering the attendants, checking again. I couldn't wait a minute longer! I had to come see him for myself. I can't get over it—I'm actually an uncle!" He reached in the cupboard for a pot. "Here, let me help with dinner," Olaf said as he filled the pot with water. The whoosh of gas ignited the stove as I flicked on the switch and placed the massive pot on the burner.

"Mom's on her way," Olaf said. "She had me bring this sauce. I swear, it's like she's got a magic freezer with endless containers of homemade sauce." He laughed, transferring the sauce into a second pot and putting in on the stove to warm.

"Coffee?" I asked.

"Sure."

We settled in the vinyl kitchen chairs and waited for the water to boil.

"So, my days are all about feedings, and diaper changes and more feedings and more diapers. Let me live vicariously for a bit! I wanna hear about your trip," I said.

"Oh, Holine," Olaf said, his eyes far off, trying to recapture the sights he left behind. "It's like no place I've ever been. Ancient and weathered and just one big beautiful mess. Some of it is tattered and just plain old—graffiti and just wear and tear. But other parts—Florence! The Ponte Vecchio! And Tuscany! You've never seen such a beautiful countryside."

"And, before Italy—you and Ted took a little jaunt to the beach?"

"Yeah, just a weekend trip," he said. "I think it's the most time I've ever taken from work, the beach and then Italy. We had a relaxing time, just wasted a few days on the beach, soaked up some rays."

"Sounds heavenly," I said.

"Yeah . . . even Bob and Tom came along," he said. "But Bob—you remember Bob? Moved to San Francisco?"

I nodded. "Graphic designer, right? Tall guy? Really friendly?"

"That's Bob," he said. "Such a great guy."

"What?" I asked, noticing a change in his expression.

"What do you mean, *What?*"

"You. You looked sad . . . or worried or something."

"Just . . . Bob. He hasn't been feeling too well." As he spoke, Olaf played around with the sugar cubes, stacking them up the way a child would stack blocks.

"What's wrong?" I asked.

"We're not sure exactly," he said, piling one cube after another on the sugar tower. "Stomach stuff . . . diarrhea."

" But—so, he's better now, right?" I asked.

"Well, he seems to get a little better, but . . . " Olaf hesitated, finally looking up at me. "It's weird . . . then it just comes back. He's going for tests, but he'd kill me if he knew I was talking about it." He put a last cube on the tower—one too many—causing it to topple.

"But what?" I asked.

"It's . . . he's also having fevers on and off," he said. "Especially at night. We're getting worried."

"I'm sure they'll figure it out," I said. "He's young. He's healthy otherwise, right?"

"Yes, but . . . " Olaf started.

"But what? Is there something you're not telling me?" I asked. "It's not serious, is it?"

"I don't know. It's just that . . . " he seemed to search for the right words. "We've heard there's this thing going around. Some mysterious illness." Olaf looked down at the sugar cubes and began to refill the sugar bowl.

"What illness?" I asked. "I didn't hear anything."

"Something the doctors can't figure out," he said. "Something that seems to be happening only to gay men. It's just . . . some of the symptoms sound like Bob's." I looked in Olaf's eyes, his eyebrows knitted in worry.

"Oh my God." I hesitated, trying to process what he was saying. Seized with sudden panic, I asked, "Wait . . . what about you? You're not trying to tell me you're sick, are you?"

"No, no. It's just . . . we're all worried about Bob." He hesitated. "To be honest, about all of us."

"Worried . . . about *everyone?*" I asked, my voice cracking.

"I mean, no one has any idea what's happening," he began, "but strange illnesses seem to be randomly attacking people, people we know. Our friend from California, Joseph—do you remember me talking about him? He's sick too. Digestive stuff, then all of a sudden, he has some kind of pneumonia."

"*Pneumonia?* That's weird."

"And Andres? Remember him? Carnegie Hall?" he began. "The guy who moved to New York? His partner is sick—something called Kaposi's." He looked away to shield me from an expression I did not have to see to understand. "Huge brown spots on his face and neck."

"But . . . I don't mean to be selfish, but what about you?" I asked, unable to mask my rising alarm. My chest tightened; my heart pounded in my ears.

The hiss and splatter of boiling water jolted us back to our surroundings. Olaf leapt out of his seat to lower the gas, but tiny puddles of salted water were already drying into murky blisters on the coppery porcelain stove. Olaf added the pasta, gave it a stir, then settled back into his chair next to me.

Looking into my eyes, he said, "I told you. I'm OK. Really. Just scared."

My breath caught. My head began to swim, just as it had the night after Paul Joe's birth, when I got up too soon without the nurses. That time, I had a call button. I gripped the side of the table with both hands to steady myself. "Now I'm scared," I said.

"I know." Olaf said. "I'm sorry, Holine. It's such a happy time for you—for our whole family. I thought about not telling you, but well, that's not us."

"No. It's not," I said. "We can never keep things from each other. Especially something this serious."

Whatever else may have been said was lost to the creak of the back door and my mother's cheery voice. "Where's my beautiful grandson?"

Olaf gave me the look that said what I already knew. She had arrived, so our conversation was over.

The red plastic ornament I bought at Eckerd drug store was cheap; still, it was my new favorite. Centered in sparkly lettering were the words, *Baby's First Christmas*. I placed it front and center on the five-foot blue spruce tucked in the corner of our living room, opposite the wood stove. The glowing fire and simple tree with its twinkling lights and popcorn strings warmed our little house. As far as I was concerned, Christmas officially started that day, the day of our annual trek west to the airport, where Olaf would be waiting in his oversized puffy coat, book in hand, beside the impossibly slow luggage conveyor at Hancock Airport. I'd waited five months for this day, and it was finally here.

Biting cold swept inside as I opened the door to the vestibule to grab my coat and mittens. I checked for mail, then gathered up the large pile of Christmas cards and catalogs and dropped it out the counter. Just as I was heading out the door, I noticed the *Newsweek* under the stack of red envelopes and shiny photos of big-eyed kids sitting on Santa's lap. I grabbed the magazine on my way out so I could read it as Paul drove.

"Man! It is freezing out!" I said, climbing into the passenger seat.

"It's not so bad," Paul answered. "The car will warm up in no time."

He turned the car onto the highway toward the New York State Thruway, headed west. I turned up the radio, pushing buttons till the jingling, sleigh-bell sounds of Christmas rang from the car's speakers. Paul looked at me as if to say, *Christmas music, again?* But he loved it too and began singing, loud and off-key, making up goofy words to verses he knew and those he didn't know.

Finally warming up, I pulled off my mittens and leafed through the magazine. I read part of an article about a Libyan conspiracy to kill Reagan. Bored halfway through, I began randomly turning pages. Midway through the magazine, past the full-page ads and feature articles and under the heading *Medicine*, bold-printed words stopped my breath: ***Diseases That Plague Gays***. The article began:

> *"An unusual assortment of disorders—some of them deadly—has recently broken out in the homosexual community. Among them: intestinal infection usually seen in the tropics, a particularly virulent strain of pneumonia and a lethal cancer most often found in equatorial Africa."*

There it was: black lettering on white pages, combining to words, phrases, sentences, paragraphs that, once written, could not be unwritten. My conversation with Olaf the previous summer always lurked in the back of my mind, nagging at me, a splinter just under the skin. Now Olaf's words came rushing back. Here it was, official, in print. It was real. My stomach lurched.

I gasped.

"Jen, you all right?" Paul asked.

"Yeah." I cleared my throat. "I'm fine."

I wanted to fold the magazine closed, to magically return it to its spot on the kitchen counter, under the Christmas cards and the catalogs. But I couldn't help myself. I read on, through two full pages: descriptions of the rapid spread of this yet unnamed disease, the words in bold print—**out of control.** The alarming statistics. And blame. Blame over promiscuity but no explanation of cause, only suspicions.

Worse yet were the gruesome details about two of the common infections, pneumocystis pneumonia and Kaposi's Sarcoma, the infection Olaf said caused the lesions his friend's partner had developed. The words swam together on the page: *"a particularly deadly form . . . which can kill within months . . . the death rates are alarmingly high."* I froze in horror at the next sentence: what was known was *"just the tip of the iceberg."*

The words dissolved into fuzzy black scribbles as dusk became dark. I shut the magazine. I said nothing as we rode through the gathering darkness, even as songs of Rudolph and holly, jolly Christmases jingled in the background.

Chapter Nine
1984

I have definitely been a victim of discrimination. I was fired from my job. I have been refused housing. Some medical care has been refused…Right now, while I'm on a research protocol at the National Institutes of Health, the government is paying for me to live in a hotel, and my medical costs are covered. However, as soon as my protocol runs out, I have no apartment to go back to. I have no job to go back to, and I am very scared about what's going to happen to me.

—Anonymous AIDS Patient, NIH video

Paul Joe roared, waving his plastic tyrannosaurus at the tiny aquilops Olaf held aloft. "*Raaaaaaah!*" Olaf jerked backwards, his face animated by fake terror. They both lay flat on their stomachs across my living room carpet, where Paul Joe brandished the T-Rex menacingly at Olaf's toy.

"*EEEEK!*" Olaf squeaked back. "Please Mr. T-Rex, don't eat me!" Olaf pulled back his measly little dinosaur and squeaked again, then attempted to hide Filo—Paul Joe's name for his favorite dinosaur—under a throw pillow "dinosaur hill."

"*RAAAH!*" Paul Joe cried again. "I'll gobble you up!" His big green dinosaur lurched forward, bumping the tiny brown Filo so hard he flew through the air, plunking me square in the forehead where I sat on the couch, folding towels.

"What the . . . " I started. "C'mon, you guys!" But it was too late; Olaf and Paul Joe were rolling on the floor, wiggling and hugging and giggling at my expense. "All right, all right. Enough dinosaur wars for one night." I wagged my finger at Paul Joe. "Time for bed, Bud-bud."

"See ya later, alligator," Olaf said. "I mean, see ya' later, juravenator," he added, like the good amateur paleontologist he'd become.

After a quick bath, Paul Joe padded out of the bathroom in his footed dino pajamas and bolted straight for Olaf's lap.

"Book time, Kiddo," I said. "C'mon."

"Uncle wead it," he said, grabbing his *Little Golden Book of Dinosaurs* from the table.

"Poor Uncle's been playing with you all day," I said.

"Uncle! Uncle!" he cried, clutching Olaf's arms.

"Well look at that!" Olaf said, faking surprise. "A dinosaur book—my favorite!" Smiling in my direction, he bent down so that Paul Joe, already climbing on the couch and still clinging to the *Little Golden Book of Dinosaurs,* could jump on his back, one arm around Olaf's neck, dangling his book by its cover with the other. As I watched them walk away, I felt the bouncing lilt of Olaf's step, the way he shifted Paul Joe on his back, and I sensed myself there again, holding him close, safe and secure, just as he'd carried me some twenty-five years earlier.

With Olaf out of the living room, I grabbed two champagne glasses and popped the cork on the split of champagne I'd hidden for the occasion. Then I poured a glass for Olaf and a glass of apple juice for myself, set them on the coffee table and waited.

"'Long, long ago, long before the days of men,'" Olaf read from the bedroom, "huge creatures . . .'"

I finished the sentence, yelling "called dinosaurs ruled the earth!"

"Your Mama!" he said to Paul Joe, "always has to get in the act." He continued his reading, and finally I heard his definitive, "THE END."

Olaf emerged from Paul Joe's room, his eyes growing wider at the sight of champagne.

"What's the occasion?" he asked.

"You're the occasion," I began. "You—and a question I've been waiting to ask."

"Well," he said, "Di fonte a chi non beve!" mimicking Grandma, who never failed to toast in Italian, *In the face of those who don't drink.* He clinked his glass against mine, took a sip, and added, "*Mmmm.* Good stuff. This *must* be an occasion."

"I'd like to invite you to a real occasion," I said. He looked at me, questioningly. "As godfather. To our new baby. Sometime next summer?"

"Godfather!" he exclaimed, beaming. "Godfather! Oh Holine . . . "

"That a 'yes'?" I asked, and he nodded, his eyes filling with tears. "No one could possibly love our kids more," I said, throwing an arm around his shoulders.

"I'm so . . . " he began. He cleared his throat. "I'm honored."

"I know the church thing may not be . . . " I began. "I know it's not easy for you."

"Well, we just won't tell 'em that I'm not worthy," he said.

"Who's not worthy?" I said. "*I* get to decide who's worthy. And no one is more worthy in my book."

"This is so . . . " he said. "Thank you, Holine." I looked into his misty eyes. "Wow. I'm gonna be a godfather," he said.

"Now," I said. "Let's talk about our trip to Atlanta this spring. It's coming up! And we can't wait to visit."

One thousand miles of snaking highways, toll booths and merge lanes; fifteen hours of staticky classic rock on the radio; one shabby Virginia motel room; five calls to Mom to check on Paul Joe, and we finally arrived in the parking lot outside Olaf and Teddy's Atlanta apartment. With another baby on the way and my due date looming, our travel window was diminishing. We knew this trip would be our last chance to visit and finally meet Teddy.

Using the handle over the truck door for leverage, I lunged out of the truck, my hip throbbing with sciatica, and hobbled up and down the pavement while Paul pulled the Samsonite from the open tailgate. I followed him through a pathway, and gasped at the sight before me: a flowering courtyard, our cobblestone passageway bordered on every side with shrubs overflowing bright fuchsia-colored azaleas, azure blue hyacinths, rows of blood red tulips and tall violet larkspur. In the center, one cement bench was supported by two blocks on either side, each adorned with ornate scrollwork. If my hip wasn't so sore—and if I wasn't aching more to see Olaf—I might have been content to sit in the midst of the lush garden, especially having left streets lined with dirty, melting April snow back home.

We arrived at 1B, and seconds after knocking, Olaf flung open the door.

"Well!" he said, "butter my butt and call me a biscuit!" He threw his arms around me, then made a groan to let me know how hard it was to reach around my growing girth. "My Holine!" he said. "How you've grown!"

"Yeah, very funny," I said, giving him a hug and a smooch on the cheek, then dropping first my purse, then myself on the couch.

"Teddy! C'mere!" he shouted. Then, turning to Paul, he said, "Brother—come in! Come in! Here—lemme put that away." He picked up the suitcase and ran down the hall, then scampered back.

"Olaf!" Paul said, pulling him in for a hug. "How the hell are ya'?"

"Good, 'specially now," Olaf answered. "*So* happy you're here!" He turned and yelled toward the doorway to a tiny kitchen. "Teddy! C'mon! They're here!"

Another door creaked and Teddy appeared, stood off to the side a moment, then stepped forward, extending his hand. "Good to finally meet you, Holine," he said.

"I've waited way too long to meet you," I replied, shaking his hand. "You're all he ever talks about." I looked into his brown eyes and remembered the photo I'd seen of him years before. He had not changed—same symmetrical features, straight nose, tousled brown hair, generous smile. Sweetly shy, he shaded his joy-filled eyes, but not before I could read his expression. He was thrilled by our visit; he knew what it meant to Olaf.

"Good to meet 'cha," Paul said, reaching out his hand to shake Ted's. Just then, a sudden movement caught the corner of my eye, and I jumped.

"What's that?" I cried.

"Oh, just Bella." Ted called. "Bella! C'mere kitty-kitty." Turning to us, he said, "Bella's a little shy." He reached down, retrieved, and then cradled the kitten, murmuring lovingly into her ear and stroking her back.

"So, Paul," Olaf began, "How was the trip?"

Paul filled Olaf in on the endless drive while I got a good look around. The apartment was a slightly larger version of the one in Geneseo, but the row of records had grown to match the room's width, extending across a several-foot-long shelf. And the piano, though slightly worn from years of use, was a newer model, not as rickety as the Geneseo piano, the one held up by a phone book under one leg. Above the one word in gold print, *Hardman*, vanilla-colored, coffee-stained sheet music was strewn across the music stand, a few individual sheets haphazardly standing on end. An enormous volume, "BACH" written in bold, ornate lettering on its cover, propped up thinner manuscripts—Haydn, Beethoven, Chopin, Verdi, and Mozart—on one side of the piano. On the other side was the five-by-eight framed photo of Paul Joe in his tiger-striped Halloween costume, a gift I'd given Olaf on his last visit home. The same old twelve-inch TV that had accompanied Olaf to college, then Chicago, and now Atlanta, was tucked into the corner on a Formica stand, its antennae looking more bent and bedraggled than ever. Piles of books overflowed on the shelf below it.

"Holine," Olaf said, taking a deep breath, "I thought you'd never get here." Then he smiled a devilish smile. "Wait till you see what I have in store! I hope you brought a dress."

"Well, since I only have two dresses that fit me," I began, "I even brought them both."

"Great," he said. "Gotta get gussied up tonight. We're going on the town! So, let's get going!"

Hoping to find my one fancy maternity dress unwrinkled enough to wear, I stepped into the bedroom where my Samsonite lay open across the bed. There, in the center of suitcase, my clothes as her cushion, sat Bella, sphinx-like, purring softly. Her eyes followed me, as though a secret was buried deep within them.

Olaf bounced into the driver's seat. Paul and Teddy jumped in the back, we headed out through the residential neighborhood, glorious with the flowering trees of spring. As if that wasn't enough to delight Paul and me, having spent the last five months looking out at walls of white snow, Olaf turned the car into an area where, one after another, the houses became grander and more ornate the farther we drove.

"Paul, look at these mansions!" I said. "We're definitely not in Central New York anymore."

"Who *lives* here anyway?" Paul asked. "There were some swanky neighborhoods in Ithaca, but nothing like this."

"Buckhead," Olaf said. "It's the cream, at least as far as Atlantans are concerned."

"I can see why," I said, gazing out at a double-balconied estate flanked by dogwoods and weeping willows. We passed stately mansions with pillared porticoes, expansive green lawns with lush manicured landscaping, circular driveways, and intricate stone facades. And one house—white stucco with red tile roof and trim, a wraparound porch and huge patio beside an Olympic-sized pool, was perhaps the grandest of all. Finally, Olaf turned the car to a more commercial section, and within minutes we arrived at a parking lot.

"Hope you're hungry," Olaf said, as he opened my door and helped me out.

One step in the restaurant, and I realized the place was much more than its understated name, *Bones*, suggested. Warm tones of gold and burgundy complemented the rich wood trim of the hallway. Olaf proudly pronounced his name and the time of our reservation, and the maître d' replied, "Very good. Follow me, Sir." He whisked us past an elevated bar enclosed with velvet curtains hung on brass dividers, then past tables adorned with crisp white linens and tasteful china plates trimmed in gold. Low lighting shone through sparkling goblets.

"Your server will be right with you," the maître d' said as he seated us at a table for four.

"Well, wha'd'ya think?" Olaf asked, smiling broadly.

"This place is . . . " I searched for the right words. "It's so *elegant*. But Olaf," I whispered, "It must be awfully pricey. Are you sure about this?"

"'Course," he said. "You're my excuse. I've been dying to try it."

"I know, but . . . " I said. "You just started your job a month ago. Really—at least let us split it."

"Not a chance!" he cried. Just then a snooty-looking waitress in a pressed grey uniform appeared as if out of nowhere, her hair in a tight bun, her posture erect as a drill sergeant's. She plucked the pencil out from behind her ear.

"Are we interested in beginning with cocktails?" she asked in a clipped, disinterested tone, then looked to the side as though we were not worth considering.

"Certainly!" Olaf said enthusiastically. He turned to us, and asked with a flourish, "Wine, y'all?" loving his newly-co-opted southern expressions. "We have to *celebrate!*" He scraped his chair closer to Teddy, wrapped an arm around his neck and gazed at him lovingly. His joy overflowing—having the people he loved best finally together at one table—he relaxed, momentarily forgetting his usual restraint.

"Feel free to peruse the wine list," said the waitress, her one eyebrow raised ever so slightly in Olaf's direction. Plunking a leather-bound folder in front of Olaf, she stalked off. I stared at her as she walked away, wondering if she had already decided that we were a bunch of insignificant hicks visiting the big city—or, if something else was behind her attitude.

Then it popped into my mind, entirely unbidden: the first TV report I'd seen about "gay cancer" months earlier.

Featured in it, Bobbi Campbell—a young man with a striking resemblance to Olaf—was described as one of several San Francisco men with a rare, puzzling illness. Tom Brokaw not-so-subtly attributed his "lifestyle" to having contracted the disease. Ever since reports like these had begun to appear on TV, whenever anyone gave Olaf even the slightest attitude, my radar went up, justifiably or not.

"Holine?" Olaf said. "Where'd you go?" shaking me from my preoccupation.

"Sorry," I said. "She was just so . . . *rude*."

"Waitzilla," Olaf murmured under his breath. Looking at Teddy, then at me, he said, "We're used to it."

After ordering a bottle of Melbac to share—ginger ale for me—and an unforgettable meal of shrimp cocktail and surf 'n turf for each of us, we lingered over cups of decaf. I turned to Olaf. "Now—tell me all about your new job. Office manager, right?"

"Yeah. For now," he said. "For the English Department." He turned to Paul, in case I hadn't told him yet. "Georgia State. Every day's a laugh riot."

"What'd'ya do there?" Paul asked.

"Little of everything," Olaf said. "Lots of typing—thank *God* for Mrs. Todd's typing class, right Holine?" He and I had had the same high school teacher, and we'd already both benefitted, job-wise, more from that skill than from just about any other.

"Made any friends yet?" I asked.

"Oh, yeah. I met this one girl, Rayanne," he said. "And you know how sometimes, you just hit it off? It's like we already finish each other's sentences."

"What's she like?" I asked.

"Real," he said. "Fun. I mean, I can say anything to her. Like you!"

"Sounds cool," Paul said.

"She's a peach," Teddy said. "Get it? Georgia? Peach?" I giggled at him.

"Teddy loves a good 'dad joke' every so often," Olaf said, shaking his head.

"No, really," Ted laughed. "Right away, it's like she's family."

"Believe me, I need a friend there," Olaf said, "if only to roll my eyes at someone when these ridiculous arguments break out."

"What?" Paul said. "What the hell they arguing about? I thought those guys just had their nose in a book twenty-four-seven."

"Oh, you don't know the half of it," Olaf laughed. "Like this one day, these two guys went at it for a half hour about the Oxford comma."

"You think they'd have more important things to fight about," Paul said.

"You wouldn't believe . . . " Olaf began, "They *love* to argue. About anything." Then, assuming his best pompous accent, Olaf began: "I *told* you, Professor Punctilious, a comma should *always* be placed after the penultimate item where it signifies a list of three of more of those items." I started to chuckle; then Teddy giggled.

"And, wait'll you hear this one," Olaf continued. "So, they're hiring another professor—someone to teach comp—and they decide they wanna appear all inclusive. So, they put this really ditsy secretary on the search committee, just to prove to HR that they're all—ya' know—liberal-minded. As if *they* really care."

"This is a good one," Teddy said, already giggling.

"So they assign this woman, Wendy, this woman who's worked there for like, a million years, to review the resumes with the professors on the committee, and, you know, they gotta read them together, right in HR, because God forbid someone misplaces a resume. And they make this matrix—a chart with the qualities they're looking for, like subject-matter expertise and publishing and all that. So, Wendy, she's reading the resumes, and she's looking kinda puzzled, but she keeps going. She gets to an application and sighs, like something's really bothering her. So finally, Dr. Barthello—he's on the committee—he says," (Olaf assumes professor voice) "'What is it, Wendy? Something you don't understand?' And Wendy goes," (Olaf does his airhead voice), "'I don't get it.' He asks her, 'What, Wendy? What don't you get?' 'Well,' she says, 'these guys all have this word *pedagogy* listed here. I don't know . . . I thought that . . . you know . . . *pedagogy* . . .'—she actually whispers this part—'isn't that *illegal?*'" Teddy starts snickering, and Paul and I look at Olaf, confused. "'*Peda-GO-GEE!*' Barthello roars, exasperated. 'The theoretical grounding for one's teaching. You're thinking of *pedophilia*, Wendy. Which is decidedly . . . different.'"

At that, all four of us lost it, our decorum shattered, disturbing not just the people at the next table, but several down the line. Like a ghost, suddenly there she was again: Waitzilla. We couldn't help ourselves, snorting and snickering like kids in trouble with the old schoolmarm.

"I assume you're ready for your check?" she said sharply.

"Yes, yes," Olaf laughed. "Sorry . . ." Waitzilla marched away in a huff, and we all broke out laughing again—all but Teddy, who'd suddenly become quiet and pale.

"Hey, you all right, Bud?" Olaf asked. "You good?"

"I . . . um . . . " Teddy began, as he grasped at the table's edge. "I . . . it's my stomach." I noticed the beads of sweat on his forehead. Teddy rose, wobbling a bit, brushing the end of the table which teetered slightly, spraying a few droplets of red wine upward from his untouched glass, tiny blotches of red staining the white tablecloth. "I'll meet you outside. Little boys' room."

"Olaf," I said. "He OK?"

"I'm sure it's nothing," he said. "Maybe Waitzilla slipped him an Ex-Lax." He attempted a laugh, but his eyes were worried.

When Olaf, Paul and I arrived at the Atlanta Dogwood Festival the next morning, it seemed to me that the whole city had turned out. Over a ridge beyond the parking lot, swarms of people filled the pathways and clustered around vendor booths, baking in the raging heat. Looking forward, we saw rows and rows of trees, bursting with blossoms of white and powder pink, complemented by rolling uphill paths thick with layers of fluffy lavender wisteria and bright pink and coral azalea.

"It's so beautiful," I said. "I don't know where to look first!"

"Miraculous, isn't it?" Olaf said. "I just love this time of year."

We walked through a paved area to a row of tents, each adorned with tastefully-displayed artwork as the artists themselves mingled with visitors and haggled over prices.

"Ah, look at this," Paul exclaimed, drawn to a selection of nature paintings, one with delicate fawns grazing below a row of evergreens so authentic, you could almost smell the pine. "These are amazing!" Paul wandered through the maze-like exhibit, while Olaf and I meandered across the way to a jewelry tent, staring in fascination as an artist weaved wire fine as fishing line into a filigreed pattern, the finished product an earring resembling a delicate leaf.

"So intricate," I said.

"Let me get some for you!"

"Oh, no, no," I protested. "Really, you gotta stop spoiling me."

"How many chances will I have to spoil you?" he said, pulling his wallet from his back pocket. "These?" he suggested, choosing a dangling turquoise and pink swirl-patterned pair.

"Oh, I love those!" I exclaimed. "Thank you." I gave his arm a squeeze and he slipped it around my waist. "Thanks, but don't wrap 'em, please," he said to the vendor. Then to me, "You *have* to wear these, right now—with your eyes—ah, perfect!" he said as I stashed my old hoop earrings in my purse and slid the new wires through my ears.

We walked back into the pathway, where Olaf spotted a bench only a few feet away. "Here," he said. "Take a load off while we wait for Paul to turn up."

"Don't hold your breath," I said. "You know him—once he gets going . . . "

"Yeah—he's a schmoozer, all right," Olaf said. "Fine with me—I hoped we'd have a few minutes to ourselves. We should talk." I waited for him to continue, but Olaf was suddenly silent.

"So…how was Teddy this morning?" Ted had left early for work before Paul and I got up.

"Seemed lots better," Olaf said. "Though he did have a night of it."

"Yeah—I thought I heard someone," I said. "You know, in and out of the bathroom."

"The rich food," Olaf said. "He seems to have developed some sensitivities. But yeah—all good now."

"That's a relief," I said. Still, I was worried. Olaf's expression didn't match his confident tone.

He paused, then said, "Tell you the truth, neither of us is feeling great lately."

"What's up?" I asked, bracing for bad news. I turned to him and looked into his face. His eyes were suddenly cloudy, and I realized they looked somehow dimmer—the whites not so white.

"I had this spell," he said. "Just exhausted, nauseous."

"Oh no! You're scaring me."

"No, no!" he said. "It's not serious. Well, it's nothing to sneeze at, as Mom would say. So, I was feeling weak, no appetite, and it just kept up. And I admit it: I was too scared to get checked out."

"I can imagine."

"Then finally one day," he said, "Teddy just insisted— you know, threatening to make the appointment for me if I didn't do it. So, yeah, I finally had it checked out. It's hepatitis."

"Hepatitis! But how?" I asked.

"Who knows?" he said. "I mean, it's a risk for gay men. And you can have it for months—years, I think—with no symptoms. So yeah, who knows."

"Wait, there's treatment, right? I mean, you'll get better. It'll go away."

"Actually," he said, "there's antivirals, but it's not like, you know, a strep infection where you take an antibiotic and it's gone a few days later. It can be chronic—or it can just go away on its own."

"But, are you OK? I mean, really?" I asked, fighting back a wave of fear.

"It comes and goes," he sighed. "Sometimes, I'm just wiped out. And there are days I just don't want to eat a thing—something I can't really afford."

"That's for sure," I said. "Oh, Olaf. As if you didn't have enough worries." I rubbed his knee gently.

"I know," he said. "But it could've been worse. Much worse."

I took his hand, and we sat in silence a moment, taking in the spectacle: people bustling in and out of tents, the park bursting with spring in all directions around them.

"Hey guys!" Paul shouted, smiling broadly and coming towards us, a brown-paper package in hand. "Wait till you see what I got!" He pulled a rectangle made of dark wood from the bag. "Ta-da!" he said, proudly revealing his treasure: an elaborate carving of a deer in a wooded meadow. Misreading our faces, he said, "Well, not exactly the reaction I was going for."

"C'mon!" Olaf said. "There's this part of the park you have to see," he declared and led the way away from the crowded vendors toward a more wooded area.

Paul helped me up, and we followed. Walking directly behind Olaf, I noticed how loosely his khaki shorts hung on him, how the bones of his shoulders protruded upward in sharp points under his lightweight Atlanta Track Club T-shirt. I shuddered.

"You OK, Jen?" Paul asked.

"Yeah," I said. "All good." But, disbelieving, he bent to look into my eyes. I shook my head. He knew better than to ask again.

Chapter Ten
1984

The good news last week was that scientists at the National Cancer Institute here and at the Pasteur Institute in Paris had found viruses they believe to be the cause of AIDS, or acquired immune deficiency syndrome, a terrifying disease that destroys the body's immune system and renders its victims helpless against infections. The discovery offered hope that screening tests and, eventually therapies will be developed to cope with the disorder. AIDS has afflicted more than 4,000 Americans, most of them homosexuals, killing about 1,750.

—Philip Boffey, A Likely Cause But Still No Cure, *The New York Times*

"The probable cause of AIDS has been found," came a woman's voice from the scratchy speaker of the portable TV tucked neatly under the kitchen cupboard. I turned from the stove, almost overturning the pot of stew bubbling on the front burner. Having assumed her serious, official demeanor, a blonde-haired, overly-coifed woman on the screen announced that, in fact, scientists had discovered the virus that causes AIDS. She went on to suggest that a vaccine would likely be developed in the next two years.

I dropped the wooden spoon in my hand and ran toward the TV to get a closer look, then cranked the volume to ensure

I'd hear every word of NBC's evening news. The woman who'd made the announcement was gone; in her place was a row of test tubes punctuated by Robert Bazell's narration, followed by a white image with a dark blob in its center. Bazell explained:

> *This is what the HTLV-3 virus looks like, magnified thousands of times, clumped on the edge of a white blood cell it's invaded. Still closer, an individual virus, showing its dense center that distinguishes it from other viruses. Gallo says a blood test for HTLV-3 will be ready in six months. It could screen out virus carriers from blood donation programs, and it could at least tell a potential AIDS victim if he or she is carrying the virus.*

I sank into a kitchen chair, my mind reeling, as I attempted to process what I'd just seen and heard. The virus— its image like an opaque stain, reminding me of the time a black Bic pen exploded in Dad's white dress shirt pocket, inky-dark at the center, a fuzzy-line border—*that* was the assassin. The words swirled in my head, crashing and colliding, generating emotions in such conflict, I sat in stunned silence trying to deconstruct what I'd heard.

It was *good* news, amazing news. A *vaccine*. In two years there might be a vaccine. Finally, it was actually going to happen—a *cure*. For three years, I had scoured the newspapers and news magazines, hoping for a shred of promise, and finally, it had come.

Yet, something in the segment nagged at me: the woman, whom I did not recognize, did not seem fully knowledgeable. Or trustworthy. She was too self-congratulatory. Something was definitely off. And that other word—*victim*—used by the reporter. I couldn't pinpoint the reason for the visceral reaction I had to that word in this context. All I knew was that it bugged me how the media continually likened sick people to criminal targets, as though a madman had selected a particular individual for the object of his crimes or a villain was out to punish people. It was a *virus*. Everyone gets them.

I pushed the negative thoughts aside. This was *progress*, and any progress was good news. There would be a blood test soon. Maybe that meant Olaf could get a test and know for certain that he wasn't infected. I had to call him, to make sure he had heard it too, as well as to convince myself I hadn't just dreamed what I heard. I pulled the kitchen phone from it hook and dialed blind, still staring at the TV in hopes that somehow I could see and hear the report again. I held the phone to my ear, let the ringing continue—ten rings, fifteen, twenty—while with my other hand I changed the channel to the CBS evening news. A reporter droned on about Libya and Margaret Thatcher, nothing about the virus. Finally I hung up the phone, half-thinking to myself that Olaf was usually home from work by that hour, half-plotting my next move.

I ran onto the front porch and snatched the local newspaper from the mailbox, furiously reading headlines and turning the pages. But there was nothing about AIDS in its meager offerings, as usual. The news was too recent, not to mention that our hometown, conservative newspaper had rarely mentioned the disease these past three years, taking its cue from the media in general.

The next day and for a few days thereafter, I scoured all the newspapers I could find in our local convenience store for an article that might confirm what I'd heard on the news. It wasn't until Sunday's *New York Times* that I found it. When I read the headline—"A Likely AIDS Cause, But Still No Cure"—my heart sank. Reading further did nothing to boost my wilting hopes. Instead, the deeper into the article I read, the angrier I became. The preponderance of the article concerned which researchers, those at the National Cancer Institute or the Pasteur Institute, were going to get credit for the discovery. And, the article made clear that Margaret Heckler, Reagan's Secretary of Health and Human Services—the very blonde-haired person I'd seen on TV days before—had overstated the development. Some scientists were backpedaling on her behalf, afraid she had raised false hopes. Worse still, researchers expressed skepticism that a vaccine could be developed in two years, if at all.

I read and reread the report, then went straight for the phone and dialed Olaf's number.

"Oh! Holine!" he said, cheerily. "I thought it might be you!"

"Olaf," I said, "I've been trying to call you for a couple days."

"What? I didn't get any messages."

"Yeah. No," I said. "No message—I just wanted to talk. You sure are a hard guy to reach."

"Yeah, I've had a week," he began. "Called in sick Monday."

"Sick?" I asked, suddenly alarmed.

"Teddy had an appointment at the clinic—just a few tests. I didn't want him going alone."

"Oh no—his stomach again?"

"Yeah, on-and-off," he said. "So finally they ordered this G.I. series. Routine stuff."

"Any results yet?"

"I mean, no," he began. "They didn't find anything—like, no ulcer or polyps or any growths or stuff like that."

"So, they're satisfied? He's all right?"

"So far," he said. "They're saying he has I.B.S.—you know, irritable bowel syndrome? I swear, that's what they always say when they don't know what the hell is happening. Anyway, more importantly, how are *you*, my little Mommy-to-be? Counting down the weeks yet?"

"Oh, I'm counting all right," I said. "I feel OK. Just big."

"Ha!" he laughed. "As it should be. Baby's gotta eat! And the Baptism? All set for the big day?"

"Yeah, it'll be low key," I said. "Just family. I only wish Teddy could come."

"Yeah. It stinks." Olaf sighed. "Story of my life. Separating my family from . . . well, my family."

"So unnecessary . . . "

"Yeah, and this stupid virus," Olaf began. "Sick or not sick—it is only making our lives a living hell."

"I know," I began. "But that's the other reason I called. I mean, other than our usual Sunday thing."

"What's up?"

"I know you've been busy, but I'm sure you've seen the news? About the virus?"

"Oh yeah," he said. "It's hard to avoid all the chatter— you know, all my friends are fussing over what it all means."

"I was pretty psyched at first," I said. "I mean—at least they know it's a virus. And they said there could be a vaccine in two years."

"Well, I know what Heckler said," he began. "I just don't think we can count any chickens just yet. Sounded like a false victory lap to me—or at least, a premature one."

"I know," I said. "She seemed too eager to take credit. But still, think of it: you could be vaccinated. It'll be like us going for polio shots all over again. All the fear and worry in the past."

"It's pretty to think so," he said. "But I'm not holding my breath."

"And the other thing—the test," I began.

"Yeah, well, I'm ambivalent there too," he interrupted.

"Why?" I said. "I mean, think of it. You could have a negative test and then put all this behind you."

"There's no putting it all behind us," he said. "Too many people lost for no good reason. And the test—there are implications. You don't know how it is. I mean, people are already losing their jobs."

"Ugh, I'm sorry. I didn't think of how the information could be used against people. It didn't even occur to me. I just want to know that you're all right. You know that."

"Of course I do," he said. "I get that you want to be hopeful. We all do. It's just that it's hard to trust when they've been ignoring us for years."

"I know. I get it."

"Hey, but listen . . . We'll just wait and see what happens. And we'll be together soon. You'll see that I'm fine, even though this wretched hepatitis is dragging me down. OK? All good."

"Yes. I guess."

"And you give me a call as soon as my Godchild gets here. I wanna be the first to know."

"I will," I said. "Love you."

"Love you too. Now, stop worrying and go have that baby!"

"The Christian community welcomes Sara Elizabeth with great joy," Father Ward said reverently. "In its name, I claim you for Christ by the sign of the cross. I now trace the cross on your forehead and invite your parents and godparents to do the same." He leaned over an expressionless Sara and motioned with his thumb, up-and-down and then side-to-side across her forehead. After leading us through responses professing our faith, the priest held his hands aloft over the Baptismal font, already filled with water, and prayed aloud. "We ask you, Father, with your son, to send the Holy Spirit upon the waters of this font. May all who are buried with Christ in the death of Baptism also rise with him to the newness of life."

I watched as Olaf loosened and removed Sara's white lace bonnet, then gently leaned her over the Baptismal font. He gazed adoringly at her, then giggled softly when she remained completely unfazed by the water that trickled down her spiky brown strands. She just widened her already round blue eyes and trained them fixedly on Olaf. Overcome, my eyes suddenly full, I rubbed his arm softly.

After the ceremony, Olaf and Mom helped me set the table and lay out the food we'd prepared the day before. The smell of homemade dough filled the kitchen, while we covered every inch of the table with homemade sausage breads and veggie pizza, antipasto with red peppers, black olives, Genoa salami, and provolone, baked pasta thick with mozzarella and spicy tomato sauce, and a wide oval tray of strawberries, pineapple, cantaloupe and raspberries. On a card table nearby, pastries from the local Italian bakery—sfogiatellle and mini cannoli and pastciotti—were nestled in dainty paper doilies on a tiered silver tray beside coffee mugs, dessert plates and matching napkins emblazoned with silver crosses.

"Looks—and smells—beautiful, Holine!" Olaf said, sprinkling ground coffee into the basket of the ten-cup electric pot.

"Speaking of looking good," I said, "that suit! You're a GQ model!"

"You like it?" he asked.

"It's fantastic! Really elegant."

"Teddy helped me pick it out for Gary's wedding— didn't I show you the picture?"

"No, I don't think so," I said.

"Here," he said, reaching for his wallet and handing me a photo he slid from a plastic sheet. "They had a photo booth. Ever see that before? The wedding photographer taking shots for the guests?" Olaf asked. I shook my head and looked at the photo, a wallet size image of him with Teddy, hand-in-hand, smiling broadly, dressed in form-fitting suits, their pressed pinstriped shirts matching the crisp pocket squares emerging from their suit pockets.

"Fabulous!" I said, and pulled the photo closer to get a better look. Teddy looked the same—tousled brown hair, warm smile—except his eyes seemed deeper set, in gaunt sockets. It was clear from his expression that he was trying to look joyful, smiling with his mouth while his eyes betrayed him. "You guys look great. I haven't even had a chance to ask: how's he been, doing?"

"He's doing OK," Olaf said. "Still some stomach issues on and off. And he wakes up at night—you know, overheated or something."

"Still?" I asked.

"It comes and goes," Olaf said. "I'd be worried, but, you know, most of the time, he really does seem OK." He saw the look in my eyes. "Honest."

Just then hoots and hollers erupted from the living room where Paul had tuned the TV to the Yankee game. Kids ran through the house, clacking their toy robots together in battle, and Olaf and I ran from kitchen to living room and back again, serving drinks and hugs to our family and friends. Sara sat on Paul's lap on the recliner—her favorite spot with her favorite person—her eyes following Mom, then the TV, then the kids, her expression placid and imperturbable, as usual. She blinked slowly, fighting sleep.

By the time the guests clustered around the door for a lengthy good-bye, I surveyed the mess. It would be hours before I got the dishes done, the house in order, the kids in bed. I turned the faucet, filling the sink with soapy hot water, while I heard Olaf wishing final good-byes to our aunts and in-laws. In the middle of the commotion, the phone rang.

"I'll get it," Olaf said, running to the bedroom phone to keep it from waking Sara, who'd fallen asleep against her father's chest, her little head barely visible above a fluffy pastel blanket.

I expected Olaf would run back out any moment, that the phone would be for Paul, as usual. When he didn't come out of the bedroom right away, I assumed he had made another call or ducked into the bathroom, so I rummaged around the kitchen, munching leftover pizza with one hand and loading glasses in the dishwasher with the other.

"Jen!" Paul yelled, "Home run!" I ran into the living room to see the replay, just as Sara awoke with a start and began whimpering.

"Nice one, Paul," I said, picking her up and taking her to the nursery where I could shut out the noise from the rest of the house.

"Sorry," he whispered after me, too late.

I stood, rocking Sara gently in my arms, and settled her into her crib, tucking the blanket around her. When I looked up, Olaf was in the doorway, his face drained of color.

"What's wrong?" I whispered.

"That was Ted," he said. "He's worse—a lot worse." He gripped the crib railing to steady himself.

"Oh, no!" I cried. The look on his face: beyond alarm, bordering on panic. His eyes wide, he dipped his head and gulped several breaths. "Here, honey," I took his arm and guided him to the rocker. "Sit. Take a breath."

"He sounded so scared, Holine." Olaf, his eyes overflowing with tears, white-knuckled the chair arms.

"What is it—same thing?" I asked. "Stomach?"

"Yeah. He called from the bathroom—couldn't even walk back to bed, couldn't catch his breath." He thought a moment. "He'd never call here . . . unless . . . he has to be really worried."

"My God!" I said. "He's alone? Can't someone go check up on him?"

"That's what took me so long," he said. "I called Rayanne. She's on her way to him right now."

"His family?" I asked.

"No . . . a definite no," Olaf said.

"Rayanne's a good friend," I said, crouching in front of him, taking his hands. "She'll help him. It'll be all right."

"I wish I could leave now," he said. "I should go. I'm gonna call American right now, change my flight." He stood, then sat again, confused.

"You have a flight first thing tomorrow," I said. "I doubt you'll get one today, this late—it's Syracuse, after all."

"I don't know, Holine," he said, and stared into my eyes. "I've got a bad feeling."

"Look—Rayanne will call and give you an update later, I'm sure of it." I looked into his sad eyes. "It'll be OK," I said, rubbing his arm softly and holding his gaze with mine. But I knew he didn't believe me. I didn't believe me either.

404-874-7471.

I dialed the number for the millionth time that Sunday afternoon. Talking on Sunday afternoons was our thing, a ritual that had become so routine, he answered the phone with "Hi, Holine," no need for caller ID. There was hardly a Sunday that passed that we didn't talk for hours. Not finding him home, by late afternoon I began to pace. I'd done all the dishes; I'd scrubbed the floor, even though it didn't need it.

404-874-7471.

I dialed one last time. Finally, Olaf answered.

"Hi, Holine," he said, sounding dejected. "Sorry—got your messages just now. I've been at the hospital all day—well, since yesterday."

"Oh no!" I asked. "What's happening?"

"It's Ted," he said. "They think it's pneumonia."

"No." I cried, dread washing over me.

"And yesterday a hideous purple spot sprouted on his forehead," he said, incredulous, struggling to grasp the reality. "Just like that."

"No!" I cried. "Not . . . Oh, Olaf."

"He's . . . " Olaf said hopelessly. "It doesn't look good." He began to cry.

"Honey," I cried, "What . . . " but I couldn't finish my sentence. I tried to focus on what he was saying, but I couldn't get any of it to make sense. Sweet Teddy. And Olaf. If Ted had it, Olaf was exposed. I felt the floor lurch, and I lost my balance, like a jolt on the subway but with no strap to grasp.

"He's so sick, Holine," he moaned, working hard to hold back his sobs. "They're testing to find out, you know . . . if it's *the* pneumonia."

"So . . . maybe," I said. "It could be just pneumonia. People get it all the time. Ma had pneumonia, remember?"

"And his fever—it's hovering around 104. One hundred and four!" Olaf cried. I imagined him sitting alone, the emptiness of an apartment usually warm with chatter and music and cooking. Of all the countless Sunday phone conversations we'd had, it was the first time I was relieved I couldn't see his face.

"Oh, Olaf," I said, hot tears stinging my eyes. I wanted to reach across the phone lines somehow, to hug it all away.

"He can barely talk," he said. "He's hooked up to all these machines. Seeing him this way . . . "

"What are they doing for him?" I asked.

"They're doing . . . I mean, they're the best," he said. "It's Atlanta. Doctor Goodson. She's seen it all before. Too many times."

"And this pneumonia—they can treat it?"

"Yeah, well," he said, "They're trying. I know he's in the best place. It's just . . .my Teddy." He began to sob harder.

"Is there someone who can sit with you?"

"I'm . . . no," he said. "I mean, yes, I'm alone but I'd rather be right now. I'm not ready to talk. Except to you."

"I wish so much . . . " I began. "You know, if it wasn't for these kids, I'd be on a plane."

"I know," he said. "But you have to stay there now. Nothing you can do here."

"And his family?" I asked. "Have you called them? I mean, you plan to?"

"I will," he said. "If . . . when we get some results. I can't think about it yet."

"It's not good?" I asked. "Between them, I mean?"

"They've never been close," he said. "I don't expect much."

"Are you sure you should be alone right now?" I asked. "I can work it out. I can get there."

"No," he said. "Not now. You need to save it for . . . later. I'm just so exhausted."

"Try to get some sleep," I said. "And keep me posted. I'm here when you need me."

"I know that," he said. "I love you, Holine. I'll call you soon."

I heard the click of the receiver.

In the silence of my house, I sat until dusk became night, the portable phone still in my hand. In the window of the house next door, a light went on; a young woman sat at the table writing on a pad. Outside, the streetlight flashed on. Somewhere far off, a siren howled, carried on the wind.

I sat in the quiet darkness, trying to comprehend what had been happening around us, all of us, for years. In the closets, under the sheets, behind drawn hospital drapes, anywhere but in the open. It had taken *knowing* someone—a real, live person. A young, promising, vibrant man. A man with a family and a job, with friends and more friends, a man with kind eyes, a perfect nose, a love for small animals, a penchant for corny jokes. A man with a partner he loved, my brother. His family, my family.

The *Today Show* blared from the TV, Jane Pauley and Bryant Gumbel chattering about the election.

"Where's my Paul Joe?" Mom called as she came through the front door. "You get over here and give your Grandma a hug!"

Paul Joe sauntered over, his "silky" wrapped around his right hand, his thumb in his mouth.

On TV, an announcer's velvety homespun voice began, "It's morning in America," while some sappy music played, like the background of a 1960's sitcom. *One more day and no more campaign ads.*

"Get that silly thumb out of your mouth!" Mom scooped up Paul Joe and teased the "silky" out of his hand. "And where is your baby sister?" she asked.

"Gwam-ma," Paul Joe said, "Come and play Legos!" He twisted himself to the ground and ran into the living room, dumping a basket full of plastic blocks in a loud, crackling crash of red, yellow, blue and green. Mom slipped off her jacket, then followed him to the floor and began stacking a rainbow tower.

"Thanks, Ma," I said. "I shouldn't be more than a half hour. Just voting and a stop to get Olaf a birthday card."

"What about Sara?" she asked.

"She'll probably sleep till I get home," I said. "But, just in case, there's a bottle in the fridge."

As I turned to leave, she smiled wryly and said, "Don't forget to vote for Reagan."

I shot her a look. "Mondale-Ferraro!" I chanted and shook my fist at her as I dashed through the door and dodged raindrops to the car.

When I returned, I spooned coffee into the filter, fired up the Mr. Coffee, and buttered bread for grilled cheese sandwiches while Mom and Paul Joe picked up the Legos. With Sara cradled in my left arm, I tested her bottle for warmth and popped it in her mouth. With my right hand, I poured coffee and a few drops of cream in each cup, a cloudy cyclone swirling on the surface. I began one-handed cutting Paul Joe's sandwich into little triangles when the phone rang.

"Hello," I snapped, sliding the phone between my ear and shoulder so I could finish getting lunch.

"Holine." It was Olaf. On a Tuesday, midday.

"Olaf? Oh, sorry, honey," I said, hoping he didn't pick up on my irritation. "Just getting lunch ready."

"I . . . I'm at the hospital," he said.

"Teddy?" I asked, dropping into a chair, Sara still cuddled in my left arm, blissfully sucking away.

"It's bad," he said darkly. "Pneumocystis. Kaposi's. He's got it."

"Mama's cwy-ing, Gwam," Paul Joe said. "Why's Mama cwying?"

Mom stared at me a moment, then dropped her face into her hands.

Chapter Eleven
1986

Everyone detected with AIDS should be tattooed in the upper forearm, to protect common-needle users, and on the buttocks, to prevent the victimization of other homosexuals.

—William F. Buckley, Crucial Steps in Combating the AIDS Epidemic: Identify All the Carriers, *The New York Times*

Click.

Buzz. Buzz. Buzz.
I banged the top of the clock.
The click alone had always been a trigger for my anxiety. My stomach lurched at the sound. I steadied myself and looked at the clock: 5:15. Time to get going.

Five days earlier, Olaf had called me from Piedmont Hospital. I knew as soon as he spoke my name, before he actually said the words. He'd said simply, "He's gone."

At Hancock Airport, I clutched my bag to my chest while I studied the departures one last time. *Flight 997 to Chicago — On Time. Gate number 22D.* No delay, no excuse to turn back.
I looked overhead, red arrows pointing me to check-in, blue to gates. My stomach rumbled and churned. I dashed into the

nearest women's room and locked myself into a stall, hoping no one would overhear me gagging and heaving.

When the second "Flight 997, now boarding!" call rang through the terminal, I no longer had a choice. I rushed to the gate and handed my ticket and driver's license to the uniformed attendant, who scowled into them and nodded me on. I followed the stragglers across the covered ramp into the plane. A wave of nausea washed over me as I inhaled the stale, dead air in the narrow passageway. I found 33B and stashed my bag in the overhead bin, then squeezed into my seat and reached up to turn the air-flow dial, hoping that if I aimed it for my face, it might lessen my queasiness. I stood to let a slight young man cross into the window seat, then settled back under the meager stream of air, gulping it greedily.

As I heard the cabin door latch, I jumped, straining against my seatbelt, overcome by the desire to run. For a split second, I was the two-year-old shut tight in a box that Olaf shoved under the bed during a game of hide-and-seek, my claustrophobia on highest alert. I looked desperately toward the aisle, unbuckled my seatbelt and stood, ready to bolt. Then Olaf's face came floating back to me. I willed myself back into my seat, took the barf bag from the seatback pocket and held it close. I closed my eyes as the plane surged suddenly forward, the momentum forcing me backward into my seat.

Breathing. The more aware I was of it, the harder it was to control. I thought back to the Lamaze method and wondered if it might work better for panicked travelers than for pregnant women. I tried inhaling slowly, then counting down a controlled exhale. But the harder I tried, the more harried and shallow my breaths became. I tried thinking of home, how I'd be back home in three days, how the whole sad episode would be over. But all

I could think about was Mom. Ted. Olaf. My stomach reeled again as we hit a pocket of air.

Almost two years had passed since Olaf called me from the hospital on election day, 1984, frantic at how quickly Ted had spiraled downward, his pneumonia raging. The day of Ted's admission, Olaf was stopped at the door by a nurse's aide. "Are you family?" she'd barked. "Family only beyond this point."

"Can you imagine?" Olaf raved. "My Teddy! Gasping for air in the next room? Alone? And I have to *beg* to get in? I was *spitting* mad! But I had to swallow it, so I wouldn't piss off those heartless *Nazis*! '*Please!*'—I was absolutely *pleading!*—'*Please! I'm all he's got!*'"

"Oh, no, Olaf. Oh my God."

"Yeah, and sick as he was, he had to sign something so they'd let me in. Then, after he's admitted, after all kinds of red tape and forms and calls to insurance, like *that's* what's important—I hear this rumble from the hallway—you know, cart noise? And this sorta clanging and a thump, and then the rumble again, fading away. So I go out in the hall. And there's this orderly, now down the hall a ways, and he's dropping trays. On the *floor*! I look down, and he *left* it! Teddy's lunch! On the grimy floor!"

"*What?* What the . . . "

"He wouldn't come in—wouldn't go in *any* rooms on the ward!" he sputtered.

"Oh, Olaf! How *could* they?"

But Olaf didn't answer. He'd begun to sob, his despair overtaking his outrage. When he finally regained his composure enough to speak he said, "The *worst* part it was how it affected Teddy. He knew that he was this . . . this . . . *pariah*. So his fever's raging, he's coughing and choking for breath, and all the while, he sees that he's considered—I don't know—less than *human*. I didn't dare leave him alone for more than an hour or two."

"I'm so sorry, Olaf. Do you want me to come?"

"No . . . no. You have your hands full—the kids, your work. Besides, you need to save it —your time off—for later."

In the weeks that followed, Olaf and I had spoken almost every day. In the first anxious days, he told me that Dr. Goodson was in-and-out of Ted's room several times a day, her laser-focus an obvious sign of her serious concern about Ted's condition. Then, miraculously, the pentamidine she prescribed started to take effect. Ted rallied. Three weeks in, he walked to the bathroom on his own. Four weeks later, he was back home.

"See?" I said to Olaf the day he gave me the good news. "You did it—you guys together. You got him home!" I summoned all the enthusiasm I could muster since, despite the good news, Olaf sounded so down.

"I know," he said. "But he was devastated when he got here."

"Why? Too much for him?"

"He wasn't even in the door yet, and he started calling, 'Kitty! Here, kitty! Where's my beautiful Bella?' I had to break it to him."

"What? Don't tell me the cat died . . . "

"No," Olaf said, his voice cracking as he struggled to stem a new flood of tears. "Doctor Goodson told me privately: 'Get rid of the cat.'"

"The cat?" I asked, still mystified.

"Apparently, it's risky, having a cat around someone with a compromised immune system,'" he choked. "The litter box . . . I don't know."

I thought back to our trip to Atlanta, how Teddy had fawned over Bella like she was his baby.

"Oh, Olaf." I said. "Losing Bella too."

"My poor Teddy. Any color he had left drained from his face. He just howled: '*Nooooooo!*' Then he turned his face from me, went into the bedroom and wept. He didn't talk to me for two days. I told him, Bella's with John and Dave. You know? They love Bella. But it was no use. He's heartbroken."

In the days that followed, Olaf began to sound more hopeful. The lesion on Ted's forehead faded, and though a few others appeared on his back, he could hide them beneath his clothes. So, when he returned to work after six weeks— weakened, twenty pounds thinner, and so tired at the end of the day, he'd head straight for bed— his co-workers just thought he'd had a bad case of the flu. He was back, sort of. A shadow of Teddy, outlined in faded ink.

Months passed. Teddy held his own long enough that the ringing phone no longer made my heart stop. Then, on a Sunday afternoon, Olaf called from the apartment. "Holine," he said, "It's . . . bad. We were just sitting here, having our morning coffee. Teddy reached for his cup, and he was, like, groping for the handle. Like it wasn't right there in front of him. Somehow, he hit the cup, and it flew sideways. Smashed on the tile, glass flying everywhere."

"What?" I asked. "I don't understand. Why?" I took the cordless and walked outside, far enough away that the kids wouldn't hear.

"Because he couldn't see, Holine. His one eye. Suddenly, he couldn't see."

"Oh my God. No."

"I begged him to let me take him to the hospital, but he insisted on staying home. He's so scared, you know, that he'll never come home again," he'd said.

Olaf and I called each other more often after that. Snatching moments during Teddy's naps to call with an update, Olaf had to endure countless interruptions on my end, inevitable with a toddler and a kindergartener as my constant companions. I rarely finished asking a question without Sara needing a diaper change or Paul Joe demanding a juice box. The kids got used to me racing from one end of the house to the other, a phone propped between my ear and shoulder while I loaded the dishwasher, folded laundry or spread peanut butter on white bread.

When Olaf and I were lucky enough to find a few peaceful moments, he kept me up-to-date on Teddy's condition. His vision was declining rapidly, leaving him no longer able to drive, and as he worsened, no longer able to read a book, to match his shoes, to dial a phone. At his scheduled appointment, the doctor mentioned new medication, but Teddy would have to qualify for a drug trial and then there was no guarantee he'd get the real thing instead of the placebo. The point became moot when Teddy's cough returned, and along with it, the fevers and chills. Teddy coughed up mucus tinged with blood, and with each hack, he had "just paralyzing pain, gasping as he held his chest." That was when Ted finally gave in, letting Olaf walk him to the car—"practically carrying him" was how Olaf described it—wrapping one arm around his waist, leading him by the elbow with the other.

"I felt like a traitor," Olaf cried, "taking him back to that place."

Teddy would never go home again.

The day my caller ID lit up, *Piedmont Hospital*, was the same day I made my flight reservation and five days before I got on the plane bound for Chicago, where I'd meet Olaf. One of Teddy's last wishes was to go home to Chicago, where his friends and family could gather to say goodbye, and where, in the comfort of his old stomping ground, he would rest forever.

I'd made the decision immediately, my response simply: "I'm coming." But even that decision was fraught with suffering. Olaf called Mom next, so when my phone rang again, it was Mom, sobbing pitifully, her regret unfathomable, her grief so deep, she could barely speak. For a boy she never met, and a son whose heart was shattered.

"Oh, Jen," she moaned, "What'll we do? My son, my poor son."

"I'm going," I said.

"I should be the one . . . " she began.

"Don't do that to yourself. I'll go."

"I want to go," she said. "But how—how can I? What would I tell your father?"

It wasn't until that moment that I realized how much she had endured on her own, sheltering Dad from her anguish over Olaf's sexuality. While she regretted the geographical distance between her and her son, she realized its necessity, for distance had allowed them both to hold Dad in the dark where he'd somehow telegraphed he was more comfortable. In the silence of her own heart, Mom had come to terms with what she could not change because her love for her son was deeper than any prejudice or stigma. But never having talked about Olaf's sexuality with Dad, she could not imagine how to tell him that his son was gay, that he'd *had* a partner, that his partner had died of AIDS. And that meant their son was exposed. Neither of us could tell him, not only because it was difficult, but because denial seemed his unexpressed preference. And the thought crossed my mind: *which of them was actually in the closet?*

"Ma, it's OK," I said. "I'll go for both of us." I could still hear her sobbing when I clicked the receiver.

I emerged from the plane and anxiously followed the crowd, which moved like one lumbering organism into the labyrinth of concourses, pathways and tunnels that is O'Hare Airport. I looked out the floor-to-ceiling windows to find the early spring weather no different from home—gray, drizzling. On an oversized TV above a row of black vinyl benches, President Reagan congratulated contra leaders on their struggle to "expel community tyranny." On the terminal wall above a line of waiting passengers, identical movie posters displayed images of a baby-faced Matthew Broderick, promoting the upcoming release of *Ferris Bueller's Day Off*. Passengers dashed forward, impatiently swinging briefcases and bursting free from clutches of travelers seeking signposts to baggage claim or ground transportation. I held back, straining to see over the rush of people, some sprinting toward gates in a furious dash to make their flights, others crashing into the arms of waiting relatives.

Then I saw him: Olaf. Glasses crooked, hair disheveled. A wisp of a man, lost inside an overcoat two sizes too big, his round, black-rimmed eyes searching. I ran to him, and seeing me, his eyes filled with tears. He collapsed in my arms. I held him for a long time as he sobbed, while travelers cut a wide swath around us, eyes lowered.

"I'm here, Honey," I whispered in his ear.

He sighed miserably, the lament of a mourning dove, then sort of gathered himself up. He seemed to summon all his energy into pulling his face back together, as if he'd just remembered where we were. He wiped his eyes on his sleeve, and stepped back to look at me.

"You look tired, too," he said. "You OK? Bad flight?"

"No," I said. "You know me. No such thing as a good flight. But I'm fine now."

"Let's get out of here," he said. "I have a car."

We walked arm-in-arm to his rental car, and on the way, he told me the plans for the weekend. A close friend from his time in Chicago, Diana, had gone to stay with her sister across town, insisting we have her one-bedroom apartment to ourselves. We'd have Friday night to rest, Ted's service on Saturday. We had synchronized our flights closely enough that we could leave together for the airport Sunday afternoon.

"Wrigleyville," he said as he drove, and, pointing forward, he exclaimed proudly, "Look, Holine: Over there—Wrigley Field. We used to sit in Diana's lawn chairs, drink beer, and listen to the cheers. Cubs fans—they're the best." His eyes lit up briefly at the memory. I realized how much it meant to him to be back in Chicago where he and Teddy had lived together for years.

I set down my bag and settled in the modest living room, breathing deeply for the first time all day. I was grateful for the space, the lumpy beige couch. I scanned the room, its walls plastered with movie posters, a black-and-white TV on a weathered bench in the corner, a green vinyl recliner, its seat cracked from wear. The place was lived-in and warm, exactly what we needed: a home instead of a generic hotel room. Olaf found some beer in the fridge of the vintage 1960's kitchenette and joined me, waving a piece of paper.

"Diana," he said fondly. "She wrote us a love note." He handed it to me: *Make yourselves at home, my sweet friends. And get a little drunk. See you tomorrow. Love, Di.* "And she left us beer and sandwiches. What a sweetheart." Olaf handed me an *Old Style* beer and sat beside me.

"So, how are you *really* doing?" I asked, taking his hand.

"It's been rough," he said. "And the next few days will be torture. If I had to do this alone . . . "

"You don't. We'll get through it together."

"I'm just . . . I'm spent," he said. "The hospital, days and days and days of it. Just endless transfusions and tests and drugs and reactions. Every day, every time I thought it couldn't get worse for him, it did."

"I don't know how you did it."

"I don't know either, to be honest," he said.

"And his family? Did they . . . " I began.

"Oh, his family," he said. "I told you they were coming, right? Just before his last admission to the hospital?" I nodded. "So, yeah, they came all right. I fixed up the bedroom—you know, where you and Paul stayed? Made them a meal that I could warm up, made brownies."

"Well, they must've appreciated that," I said.

"No, you don't understand. They not only didn't appreciate it. They didn't stay." Tears welled in his eyes.

"Didn't stay? What?"

"They got a hotel!" he said, his voice shaking. "Wouldn't touch a bite of food. Ted's father—he came in with gloves on. *Gloves.* You know, the kind doctors wear."

"*What?*"

"It was so obvious," he fumed. "They thought they'd get it too. That's what they cared about: not getting AIDS."

"Oh my God." I shook my head in disbelief.

"They stayed with him, for what, I don't know . . . forty minutes?" he said, as the tears he'd been fighting trailed down his cheeks. "Forty minutes. With your son. Who is dying. Can you imagine?"

"It's unspeakable," I said, handing him a tissue and gently rubbing his arm.

"Oh, it gets worse," he said. "They barely spoke to me."

"What?"

"They blame me, Holine." Olaf buried his eyes in his hands, shaking his head sadly. "They *blame* me."

"No, no," I said. "Don't let them do that to you. Don't even think about that." I slid closer and put my arm around Olaf. He looked up, struggling to regain his composure, yet another single tear escaped the corner of his eye. I took his chin in my hand, lifted his face and looked into his eyes. "It's a virus. No one's fault. I know how you loved him. How you'd never hurt him. It's not your fault."

"They'll be there tomorrow," he said. "When I say good-bye to Teddy, they'll be there, blaming me."

"Don't," I said. "Everyone knows how you cared for him. And, where were they? Don't do this to yourself."

"I know," he said. "It's just . . . "

"Here," I motioned to his beer. "Take a sip. And let's get you something to eat."

"I should eat, I suppose," he said.

"And after that," I said. "Sleep. You probably haven't slept in years. Literally."

"I guess."

"And you're taking the bed," I said, summoning my best "mom" voice.

"OK, Holine," he said, reluctantly. "I know you're right."

"Maybe if you get some sleep, you'll feel better. Even a little. C'mon."

I led him to the kitchen where we stood at the counter, eating, if not tasting, the sandwiches. Then I marched him off to bed, kissing him lightly on the top of his head, wishing I could find a word—a magic word—one that would make him forget, just for a moment. But no magic word came to me. No word at all.

Finally, snuggled under an afghan on the lumpy couch, I drifted off to a dreamy sleep.

"Do you see any yet?" I called, trailing behind Olaf, unable to keep up with his pace.

"Nope," he yelled back. "No frogs here. C'mon."

I walked behind Olaf along the stream's bank, tracing his footsteps through the underbrush and around stumps and fallen branches. The air was heavy with the smell of wet earth and worms tangled in squirming knots; muddy sludge and leaves squished under my ratty sneakers.

Olaf stopped, poked his "walking stick" under a rock, so I stopped too and opened my rinsed-out pickle jar, just in case.

"Nah," he said. "Just worms." He waved me forward and started up again, me behind, toward some thick undergrowth at the water's edge. He stopped, bent to inspect some brush beside a jagged flat rock.

"C'mere!" he shouted. "You gotta see this!" I ran up behind him on my squatty, seven-year-old legs, just as he dipped his stick under a bush, then raised it triumphantly, "No frog, but . . . better!" he exclaimed. Hanging from the end of his stick was a gray, sleeve-shaped object.

"What?" I said, finally getting close enough to see it. "What is it? Looks like a dried-up old sock or something."

"A snakeskin!" he cried. "Look close. You can still see the scales." His eyes wide, he gazed into and around it, as if it was some kind of miracle. "Can you imagine? A real live thing was inside it." He thought a moment, and his eyes drooped sadly. "All that's left of this poor little guy. An empty shell."

"Yeah," I said. "But the snake—it's really still alive somewhere."

"I know," he replied. "But to think, this was a real live thing. Now it's not."

I shot up in bed, trying to remember where I was. The snakeskin. Olaf's eyes. I shook my head, looked around the room: the movie posters, the TV, the green chair. Diana's. I was at Diana's, and today Olaf and I would go to Teddy's funeral. But the dream: it was still there too, hanging, as sure as the dusty curtains that sagged from a bent rod over the apartment window. It would follow me like a shadow all day.

A few hours later, after three cups of very strong coffee, Olaf and I took off on foot to meet Diana and her partner at Dinkel's, a bakery-café Olaf loved because it was "the real deal . . . you know, old school." Turned out it was one of those places that was cool once, uncool for a while, then cool again, a retro haven. Just past the entrance were rows and rows of glass-encased Danish pastries, apple fritters, bear claws, and delicate cookies with lemon and chocolate and raspberry icing—even a doughnut with the Cubs logo sketched in red, white, and blue frosting. Loaves of bread were stacked to the ceiling: sourdough, Italian, French baguette. And the smell: rising dough, sweet sticky cinnamon buns, butter melting over crusty bread browning in gas ovens.

As we rounded the corner, Olaf dashed to the side of a table where three young women sat, oblivious to us, their heads together in whispered talk like co-conspirators plotting their next heist. Two of them looked like they could be twins: cropped brown hair over bushy eyebrows and inviting blue eyes, buttons for noses. The other was a long-haired blonde with a flawless complexion, almost invisible eyebrows, blue-green eyes, a perfectly-sloping nose. One of the cropped-haired women glanced up, sensing someone approaching. She let out a yelp, jumped up and threw her arms around Olaf.

"You're here!" she cried. "Man, buddy! I've missed you!"

"Me too, Di. Me, too," Olaf said, giving her a tight hug and a kiss on the cheek.

"You OK?" she said, looking deep into his eyes.

"No," he said. "But better now, seeing you. Oh, and my sister's here. This is Jennifer."

"Good to meet you," I said. "And thanks so much for giving up your apartment. Just like home."

"Aww," she said. "It's not much, but we like it, right, Steph?" Stephanie, the blonde-haired woman nodded politely, then held out her hand to shake mine.

"How ya' doin'?" she said, and then motioned toward the other woman. "And this is Debra, Diana's sister."

"Good to meet you," I said. Olaf went around the table and shook her hand.

"Sit, guys, sit," Diana said. "And, I know you've got a time crunch, so let's order. Anyway, I'm starved. You guys gotta try the chicken salad on six-grain bread—it's the bomb."

After the waitress took our order, Dianna turned to Olaf.

"So, it's been rough, huh, kid?" she said, taking Olaf's hand in hers.

"Yeah," he said. "Just torture. No words for what Teddy went through."

"I know," she said. "We were so sad that we didn't get to see him. Not a day went by that I didn't wish you guys were still in Chicago. I could've helped you. Or just . . . been there."

"I'm sorry you missed seeing him," Olaf said. "You and Ted—you were so special to him. Oh, and I have something. Here, he wanted you to have this." He dug in his pocket and pulled out a small ring, a tiny silver baseball glove hanging from the end. "His Cubs keychain."

Diana's eyes welled up, and she hesitated, holding back tears. Then she laughed softly, "Remember? The day the foul ball almost clunked him on the head? Klutz. I used to tell him, 'You couldn't catch a cold.' Wish I'd been right." She reached in her bag to get her keys, removing them one-by-one, replacing them on Ted's keychain. "So, you're here, at least you're here now," she said. "And your sister too. How great to have her with you."

"She's my rock," Olaf said, nodding in my direction.

"She looks a little like your mom," Diana said.

"Really?" Olaf said, surprised. "I—oh yeah—I forgot you met Mom when she came to visit us that time."

"Wait—what?" I said.

"Ma," he began. "Remember? She came to Chicago, all by herself. Her olive-branch visit. You know."

"I still remember her," Diana said. "She was so cute, Steph, you remember? Just this petite, sweet-faced, gentle person. And her clothes. Everything matched, even her lipstick. But you could tell, she was a spitfire once you got her going."

"Yeah," Olaf said. "A coupla times, I saw her . . . you know it, Holine—her Bette Davis face? Like she was not having it. Not at all," he laughed.

"I didn't get that about her," Diana said.

"That's because, really . . . " Olaf began, "Most of the time she was here, she was so sweet, so accepting, so willing to do whatever. She really tried. I couldn't believe she even came."

"Yeah, she was fun," Diana said. "Very polite, but not in a phony way. Not like some of the moms who put up a front."

"Yeah!" Stephanie piped up. "I remember now. She was a tiny little thing. Really cute. And she made that scrunched-up face when she didn't like something—the same one you make!" she said, tapping Olaf's wrist.

"We get that a lot," he said.

"But she was a trooper. Like, determined to be a good sport," Diana said.

"I know it was hard for her, meeting all my wayward friends," Olaf chuckled, rolled his eyes. "But sometimes she'd look at me, questioning, like, was it too late? But no, it was never too late."

"Wow," I said, "We really never talked about it much. I mean, she said she loved Chicago and your friends and all, but that's about it."

"It was that she came at all," Olaf said. "She didn't have to mouth the words. Her being here, that was everything."

"Deb," Diana said, "Tell 'em about our mom."

"Oh, our mama," she said, her round eyes growing wider. "She's a hoot. Doesn't care who we sleep with, just so long as we bring her vodka every Sunday. Starts drinking soon as she's home from church."

That set everyone off. Olaf grinned at me. "Can you imagine? Ma drinking at 11 a.m. on Sunday after mass at St. John's?"

Just then, the waitress slapped our check on the table, smiling at our merriment, probably imagining a simple reunion of friends, not a prelude to a funeral.

"I got this," Diana said.

"No, honey," Olaf said. "You've done enough."

"I wish," she said. "Now, if only I could turn back time."

Two men in three-piece suits paced on the sidewalk in front of the funeral home, smoking madly, as if in a contest to finish first. As we approached the door, another dark-suited man appeared and held it open.

"Evening," he said soberly. "This way."

A whoosh of warm air escaped the doorway, dragging with it the sickeningly sweet fragrance of too many flowers in too small a space. Olaf grasped the railing as he slowly climbed the vestibule steps. He looked back at me.

"Hang on to me," I said, and took his arm.

I scanned the room: a leather-bound book for mourners to sign; prayer cards bearing the words, *Lord, Make Me An Instrument of Your Peace,* Olaf's favorite prayer; boxed tissues on a side table beside a stemmed dish of hard candies; a cross of roses on a mahogany box, a kneeler set before it; a low murmur rising from a group of five clustered in a front row of chairs; classical music, barely audible, as if piped from the heavens.

One of a small group of mourners approached Olaf. "Teddy's cousins," he said, reaching out his hand to shake Olaf's. "We're so sorry." The others nodded their acknowledgement. "We loved Teddy so much." Olaf looked at him gratefully, touched by acceptance and love, as the man pulled him in for a hug.

"My sister, Jennifer," Olaf said. I shook hands down the line.

The door opened again, and in rushed Diana and Stephanie, passing right by the guestbook. They embraced Olaf and kissed his cheeks, now streaked with silent tears.

A grandfatherly man in a cleric's collar appeared and reached out to Olaf. "Here you are," he said. "Ok? Ok now," he patted Olaf's hand nervously and led him to the kneeler. I followed, stood behind him, my hand on his shoulder.

So many young men had grown prematurely old, gray-haired and gray-faced, time passing for them at warp speed. Ted was not one of them. He seemed to have grown younger, his fair face childlike, a baby bird in too large a box.

Finally, Olaf rose. The minister ushered us to seats along the side, closest to Teddy. I pulled a tissue from my pocket, took his hand, and waited.

Cool outside air wafted through from the entrance. Olaf gave a low gasp as an older man guided a stern-looking woman by her arm toward the kneeler. They stood behind it for several minutes, staring forward, stone-faced, until the woman broke down. She looked helplessly at the man, who guided her to chairs along the perimeter. Neither looked in our direction.

I looked into Olaf's stricken face, his words from my dream coming back to me: "All that's left of this poor guy. An empty shell."

With some time to kill before our flights, Olaf and I headed out for a walk so he could revisit his old neighborhood. We strolled down Waveland Avenue, past rows of one-family houses with tidy, white-railed porches overlooking oaks and maples, just about to bud. Wayne, Southport, Jansen—we passed several side streets, then made a few more turns. In no time, I was completely lost. Olaf walked briskly but silently, determinedly, taking in the sights.

After a few blocks, he said, "C'mon, Holine—this way." And we turned again, coming to a four-story, U-shaped red brick complex with a weary courtyard in its center, slightly overgrown bushes lining the perimeter. Wrought-iron tables and chairs were randomly placed around the grounds, a few of the chairs overturned. Patches of rust were visible in spots beneath the tabletop's peeling paint.

As he entered the courtyard, Olaf stopped short and stared straight ahead. He began to weep.

146

"Olaf! Oh, Honey." I rushed to his side.

"It's OK," he said. "It's just, we lived here, me and Teddy. Our first apartment in Chicago." He walked further, and finding a sturdy chair, sat, his face in his hands. Then, looking up at me, he mumbled, "I'm sorry. Is this too morbid, Holine?"

"Of course not," I said, crouching in front of him, taking his hands, seeking his eyes. "I understand."

"It's just . . . till you see it again, it's like . . . maybe you dreamed it. But no, it was real. We were here, me and Teddy."

"I know, Honey. I know."

"I don't know what I'm going to do," he sighed hopelessly, and dropping his chin to his chest, he cradled his forehead in his hand. "Holine, what am I going to do?"

No answer came to me. I pulled a chair beside him, and we sat in silence.

At the airport, we got to Olaf's gate first, since his flight was an hour earlier. He rummaged in his bag, fiddling with his ticket, placing it in the book he'd brought to read on the plane, then changing his mind, returning it to his pocket. When the boarding call came, he looked straight into my eyes.

"Holine, I can't . . . " he began, his voice raspy, he stopped in mid-sentence, fighting off another flood of grief.

"I know," I said. He hugged me tightly, then turned, never looking back. "Love you!" I called after him. "Call you when I land."

I knew that the wisest thing would be to hurry to my gate. But I couldn't move. I stood at the window and waited. Minutes ticked by, as the line of boarding passengers dwindled to one final traveler, sprinting his way to the passage, fumbling for his ticket. The sky was just beginning to darken when the plane glided ever so gently forward, then picked up speed. It taxied down the runway and lifted gracefully, angled toward the sky. I watched it shrink gradually in the distance until it faded behind a cloud, leaving only a streak of gray in its wake.

Chapter Twelve
1987-1988

There is no question on the part of anyone fighting AIDS that the F.D.A . . . is actually prolonging this roll call of death. This has been only further compounded by President Reagan, who has yet to utter publicly the word "AIDS" or put anyone in charge of the fight against it.

—Larry Kramer, The F.D.A.'s Callous Response to AIDS, *The New York Times*

"Kiddo!" Olaf's voice rang through the receiver. "I couldn't help myself! Dialed your number the minute I got home. Tell! I wanna hear everything!"

"Oh my God, Olaf!" I said breathlessly, having dashed to the ringing phone just as I burst through the back door. "It's *perfect*."

"So, the tutoring—is it just writing or . . . "

"Yup, writing tutoring. I have my own office in the Learning Center—well, I call it an office, even though my closet is actually bigger—but, it's *mine!*"

"Hey! It's a start," he said.

"Yeah, and it means I get to teach all day, without having hours of prep or papers to grade."

"Wow—sounds just *made* for you right now," he said.

"I can even pick up an ESL writing class, which'll be great—having one class of my own, too. And what about you? It must be good to be back teaching at good old Macintosh High, huh?"

"Hilarious, as usual," he said. "I swear, Holine . . . these kids are so funny. And even though four preps are killer, I'm psyched about the senior lit class. It's a dream," he said. "But tell more about you. What else?"

"Well, my new colleagues, Ellis and Marie—you would love them. I mean, I actually got thinking—these are people *you* would've chosen as friends. They're so smart and all about the students—like you."

"How great for you—a new job *and* new friends," Olaf said. "After all those years mommy-ing at home—to be with adults again."

"Yeah, it's great, except . . . "

"Oh no—don't tell me," he said. "Someone already bugging you?"

"No, no, not *someone.* More like *something.*"

"What'd'ya mean, *something?*"

"Well, so after lunch, we all had to file into this huge auditorium—I mean, probably as big as the theater downtown, I'm not kidding. And, I didn't realize, seriously *hundreds* of people work at this place. So, I'm sitting there with Ellis and Marie on either side of me, and you know, they're exchanging glances, just rolling their eyes while the college president, he's just going on and on about enrollment and strategic goals and development—I mean, *on and on and on.* But then, he starts introducing all us newbies."

"But that's good, right? So you'll know who else is just starting. You know, another way to meet some young professional types?"

"Yeah, I guess," I began. "But I couldn't even think about that. All of a sudden, it was like . . . I don't know . . . like I might *faint* or something. I just . . . when I knew he was going to talk about me, my heart just about jumped out of my chest. I felt the heat rising in my face, which had to be beet red. Everyone musta wondered what the hell was wrong with me. For a split second, I thought I might bolt. Boy, did I want out of that room."

"Huh," he said. "Probably just first-day jitters."

"It didn't feel like simple jitters . . . I don't know."

"Well, you survived, right?" he asked. "I mean, you didn't have to *say* anything?"

"No," I said. "That's what's weird. Just being introduced and having to stand up while everyone gawked at me—it was so embarrassing."

"I'm sure once you get to know everyone better, those meetings will be a breeze. You'll be rolling your eyes along with your new friends in no time," he laughed. "And speaking of eye-rolling, how did my too-cool-for-school goddaughter do on her first day of preschool?"

"Just as we thought," I said. "Only better. Not only *didn't* she cry or carry on when it was time for me to leave, she just about shooed me out the door. 'You can go,' she said, dismissing me, you know—like I was cramping her style!"

"That's Sara," Olaf laughed. "Can't say I'm surprised."

"And you? What else are you up to? Choir tonight?"

"No. Tonight it's Italian practice with Maria, choir practice tomorrow, language club Thursday. Then we have Parents' Open House next week."

"You are one busy Olaf! I get tired just thinking about it," I said.

"It's good for me," he said. "I—uh—I do better when I'm not here . . . You know, it's tough in the apartment, without Teddy. Everywhere I look, there's something—his college mug and now, one of Bella's kittens. At least I've stopped wearing his sweatpants to bed."

"I know, Honey. Or, at least . . . I can imagine."

"Anyway, there isn't one thing— the teaching, the rehearsals, performances, none of it—that I don't love doing, and it feels good to be busy. I *do* wish I could fit in more sleep, though."

"You better take care of you," I said.

"I know," he said. "I will. Promise."

My new colleagues and I, along with our regular student visitors, became a little family, one that I looked forward to seeing every day. My days were filled with back-to-back appointments, so work days passed quickly as more and more students appeared with questions about sentence structure and grammar, thesis statements and verb agreement. My favorite students were refugees from Vietnam, Belarus and Cambodia—all of whom, without fail, bowed reverently as they backed their way out of my office at the end of a session—and a band of tiny 19-year-old Japanese students, computerized language translators peeking out from the pockets of their identical oversized backpacks. Some students checked in daily, like my Belarusian friend, Peter Brutsky—one of my favorites—who'd poke his head in to ask such questions as, "What means *whatzup?*"

Still, that stressful first faculty meeting kept crossing my mind. As the next meeting day approached, my stomach began to churn. When I arrived, I sat as close to the door as possible, knowing I'd feel the urge to escape, even while I suspected I'd somehow hyperventilate my way through it, never drawing attention to myself by actually running. Within minutes of the call to order, I was overtaken by a blend of weakness and nausea, on the edge of fainting. My heart pounded in my ears, my palms became sweaty. Objects and people around me took on a surreal quality, a shimmery muddle of dissolving lines. I sat with my head bowed, counting the minutes till it was finally over.

Olaf and I kept up with each other's lives by phone, just like the old days before Teddy got sick, but, with Olaf's schedule, our calls had to wait until Sundays. I could always tell by his tone whether he was having a blue day—usually when he was alone in the apartment for too long, his "Hi, Holine" sounding more like an exhale than a greeting. However, most days he sounded exhilarated, excited by a piece of music or a productive day in the classroom. Yet every so often I detected a hint of forced enthusiasm followed by a few beats of uneasy silence, as if, should he stop talking—or moving—his momentum would be broken.

One particular Sunday late in the school year, I'd barely finished dialing when he picked up, breathless and excited.

"Holine!" he shouted, "I was just about to call you! I am out of my mind!"

"What's happening?" I said, tucking the phone between my right ear and my shoulder, while I slid dirty dishes into the sudsy water.

"I got in! I got *in!*"

"What?" I asked. "Got in where?"

"Middlebury!" he said. "You know, MIDDLEBURY! The Italian program! I actually got in!" I turned the water off to make sure I heard him correctly.

"Oh Jeez!" I said. "Wow! That was fast, right? So when you start?"

"Last two weeks of May," he said. "There's so much to do! But, can you believe this? I tested into level three—level three! Just by studying Italian with Maria in the evenings. So, after eight weeks at Middlebury, I'll be almost to bachelor's level."

"What? Already?"

"Yeah—and if all goes well, I can go again next summer and have my master's in one year. Then I'll be able to actually teach it! Italian!"

"That's crazy!" I cried. "That's gotta be some kind of record! Nobody learns a language that fast." I picked up my sponge, and started on the dishes.

"But wait! There's more! After Middlebury, I am going . . . TO EUROPE!" he screamed.

"WHAT! Oh my God! How? Who with?"

"A couple of teachers from school—we got talking and we thought, why not? Summer is so long, why not take a month and spend it abroad? Just think of what we'll bring back to our classrooms! It couldn't be more perfect. Eight weeks of language immersion, then conversation with *real* Italians. I can't even believe it myself!"

"Sounds heavenly," I said, giving up on the dishes and plunking myself into a kitchen chair. "I can't even imagine. But does this mean you won't have time to come home this summer?"

"That's another bonus," he said. "I can get the train home from Vermont for a week before Europe, and I'll still have another week to spend with you guys before school starts again. It's perfect."

"That's a relief—it wouldn't be summer if I didn't get to see you. Sounds like you thought of everything. Wow, Olaf — it's all so exciting! You're actually doing this!"

"Get it while you can—that's what I say!" he said.

The words rang in my ears after we'd hung up, familiar somehow. I later realized they were the lyrics of an old Janis

Joplin song we'd played countless times, together belting out her warning as it floated over us from Olaf's speakers: *We may not be here tomorrow . . . Honey! Get it while you can!* Janis had warned us — Janis, who'd squeezed as much living as possible into her 28 years, as if sensing her fate.

Postcards from all over Europe began to arrive at our little upstate New York home. I raced to the mailbox every day, hoping for a way, mentally at least, to put a pin in the world map. I had to know where Olaf was, to know he was *somewhere*. We'd only been this far away from each other one other time, the year Paul Joe was born, but that was only for ten days. This time, his trip was three whole weeks.

The first postcard to arrive was a photo of the Galleria Vittorio Emanuele in Milan, a compound of stately buildings with awning-adorned arched windows over colorful shop fronts connected by an ornate glass-and-iron vaulted arcade. The great bowed ceiling was intricately laced with rectangle cutouts, like a child's homemade valentine that, once unfolded, reveals an intricate pattern. I had never seen, nor could I have dreamed such a place.

I could hear his voice as I read, his perfect Italian pronunciation of *Ciampino Aeroporto*. I read and re-read, turning the words over in my head. *Layover. Wait. Hot. Dirty. Expensive.* The words alone made me anxious. But Olaf saw his trip as a big adventure, his adrenaline pulsing, pushing him towards something—possibility. Even as Olaf seemed to dash forward in his life, I was experiencing a different type of adrenaline, the kind that starts like a match tossed into a gasoline pool at your feet, a lifeforce that blazes its way up your legs into your belly, shouting, *Run!* And I wondered if Olaf was running too, from his lonely apartment, his sadness and grief.

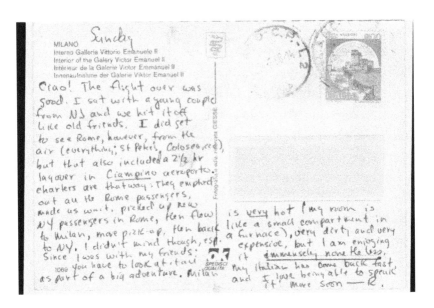

Four days later, another card arrived from Milan, a baroque cathedral pictured on one side. On the back, Olaf had written words that suggested I might even lose him for good to his newly-adopted country.

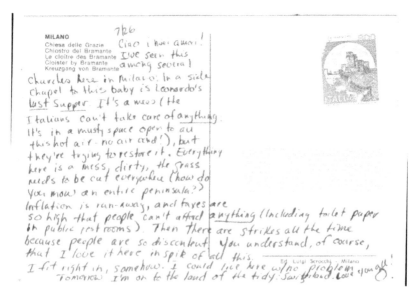

MILANO
Chiesa delle Grazie
Chiostro del Bramante
Le cloître des Bramante
Cloister by Bramante
Kreuzgang von Bramante

726

Ciao i miei amici!
I've seen this
among several
Churches here in Milano: In a side
chapel to this baby is Leonardo's
Last Supper. It's a mess (the
Italians can't take care of anything.
It's in a musty space open to all
this hot air - no air cond!), but
they're trying to restore it. Everything
here is a mess, dirty, the grass
needs to be cut everywhere (how do
you mow an entire peninsula?)
Inflation is run-away, and taxes are
so high that people can't afford anything (including toilet paper
in public rest rooms). Then there are strikes all the time
because people are so discontent. You understand, of course,
that I love it here in spite of all this.
I fit right in, somehow. I could live here w/no problem enough!
Tomorrow I'm on to the land of the tidy: Switzerland. Love you

Ed. Luigi Scrocchi - Milano

Olaf had purchased a Eurail pass. This allowed him to
travel freely throughout Europe to all of the places where his
heroes had once created the music he so treasured: Schubert,
Beethoven, Brahms, and Mozart. Cards arrived almost daily,
vivid color photos of majestic churches and opera houses. I
imagined a dizzying itinerary that took him from Italy to
Switzerland, Germany, Austria and back to Italy.

Then a postcard arrived from Florence, the city which
captured his heart. So many cities, so much motion, so much
culture squeezed into so little time. I thought, "*Molto allegro! Molto
allegro!*" remembering the words his music teacher shouted

during Olaf's lesson, clapping his hands in rhythm when Olaf played too slowly. I wondered if, all those miles away, Olaf was hearing his voice too, urging him forward: *Faster. Faster.*

At night, I felt Olaf's frenetic pace as I tossed in my bed. I felt him tapping a nervous foot against the train platform, heard his fingers drumming against a taxi window. When I finally slept, I *dreamt* of Olaf. Olaf in all the postcards—kneeling in a Milanese

cathedral, perched on the Spanish Steps, leaning on the ledge of the Ponte Vecchio. Riding in a rickety Italian bus . . .

> *The bus was packed with wayward travelers, belting Italian folksongs with full-throated glee. One particularly boisterous songster reached across the aisle, his fist wrapped around the narrow neck of a bottle—the kind with the basket-weave bottom—red wine sloshing in rhythm with the bus's motion. The traveler attempted to fill the plastic glass of a passenger across the way. It was Olaf! Olaf, his glass in his outstretched hand, his mouth wide in happy song. But the bus, speeding too fast around the cliff-hugging road, lurched around a bend, sending a stream of red wine onto his white*

linen shirt, streaking it with red. Olaf laughed heartily as he shook off the bloody droplets that trickled down his hand. "What's a little wine?" he shouted, then launched into song once again while the man across the aisle managed to pour what was left into his cup. As the bus rounded the curve, Olaf lost his footing, and tried to right himself. No sooner had he recovered his balance when a miniature Fiat crossed the center line as it barreled around a bend, headed straight toward the bus. Brakes squealed. The bus veered suddenly, blasting into the guardrail before sailing over the cliff.

The impact jolted me upward. I tasted the salt in Olaf's mouth. Was it he or I who had been crying? I blinked, startled. The next day a postcard from Salzburg arrived:

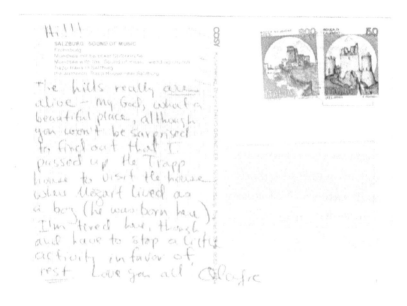

Of course he's tired! All that moving from place-to-place. But I couldn't help wrestling with the idea that a 36-year-old man in the prime of his life in the place of his dreams had to stop and rest.

As soon as Paul got home from work, I showed him the Salzburg postcard.

"Do you think he's really OK? Do you think he's doing too much?"

"Jen," Paul said. "He's *fine*. He's just tired from all the travel. Who wouldn't be?"

"I don't know . . . "

Paul just shook his head, looked into my worried eyes, and sighed.

My first ever professional conference was that spring, an event I had been urged to attend with new colleague, Marie. Before the keynote dinner, I wandered through the ancient Catskill resort, stopping in at the cocktail hour. China snack plates in hand, conference-goers piled delicacies from the long banquet table spread with generous platters of cheese and fruits, shrimp hors d'oeuvres, mushroom canapes and spinach-stuffed pastries. A crescendo of pleasant chatter and clinking glasses rose throughout the room as colleagues who once worked together caught up with old friends who'd ventured elsewhere, vaulting through careers. As I surveyed the banquet table, my stomach flipped at the garlic-seafood aroma, a wave of nausea catching me off guard.

Then, without warning, the room faded out. Then in. Then out again. All I could think was: *Run*.

I tripped past clusters of high-top tables toward the ladies' room, the floor rising under my feet.

I crashed into a restroom stall, slithered down the metal wall—clammy, like my hands—till I was sitting on the cold linoleum, my head between my knees. I hugged them tightly to my chest, trying to stop myself from shaking. The outside door creaked.

"Jen? You OK?" Marie's voice floated from behind the door.

"I . . . I'll be OK," I muttered from behind the door. "I'm so sorry. You go back, please. I'll be out in a minute."

"Are you sure you're OK?" she asked. "Can I do something? Bring you something? Water?"

Minutes later, she slid a glass under the door.

"What's going on? Any better?" she asked.

"I think so. Please . . . please . . . " I began. "Go back. I'm really OK."

"You are *sure*? I don't want to leave you like this," she said.

"I'm good. Really. I feel better already."

"If you're absolutely certain . . . " she said.

"You're a good friend," I said. "Now go back. Please—it's OK."

"Ok," she said tentatively. "But I'm coming to check on you!"

Finally, my breathing slowed, the world realigned. The funhouse through which I had faltered regained its structure—the floor had leveled, the walls resumed solidity. I wanted to be a woman at the conference, to see the room as a room, to converse with other educators, to learn from them. But I just couldn't do it. I could not go back. The earth had a way of sending me reeling. I did not trust it.

I got up, splashed water on my face, and seeing myself in the mirror—the pale of my lips, the beads of sweat on my forehead—I knew that I was very, very sick. Maybe it was my heart, or a stroke. I had to get to a doctor. I rushed back to my hotel room, and slumped onto the bed. Still shaking, I reached for the phone and called Paul to come and get me. When I was finally able, I tossed clothes haphazardly into my suitcase, wrote Marie a note, and took off toward the elevator.

In the half-light just outside the hotel's back entrance, I waited for Paul. The only sounds were the clacking and whirring of insects overhead. One solitary bulb covered by a glass sconce hung above the doorway. Inside it, a cluster of angry moths jostled in pattern-less flight and banged against the glass.

Paul's truck screeched around the corner and pulled up in front of me. I was in the passenger seat before the truck rolled to a stop.

The next evening I sat, fully clothed, on the toilet seat, cover down, my head between my knees. I tried to slow down my breathing and still the swimming in my head. Light became dark. Struggling to center myself, I reached sideways, turning the faucet handle to run cold water. I laid my forehead against the sink's cold porcelain.

"Jen? You all right?" Paul asked from the other side of the door.

"Yeah," I said, in the most normal voice I could muster.

"You sure?" he asked. "You been in there forever."

"I said I'm fine," I replied, a little too firmly, realizing as I heard my own voice that I might sound very un-fine. Footsteps became fainter as he walked away down the hall.

The kids. I have to go watch the kids. They would be at the door any minute now, knocking and calling for Mommy. It was getting close to bedtime, time for baths and books and prayers. But my feet were immovable, cast in concrete. In the living room, Fozzie Bear and the Muppet band continued playing silly songs. I still had a minute, maybe two.

The four-by-five foot bathroom was tucked away in the back of the house. The only way to reach it was through my bedroom. The vinyl floor was a mere twenty-inch deep path, barely room enough for one person. Although the bathroom door had no lock, I had pulled the cabinet drawer open, sliding it across the closed door so that it could not be pushed from the outside. I had pasted on my Mommy face for the entire day, so long that it ached.

Heavy footsteps grew louder as Paul returned toward the bathroom. "Jen! Seriously! Are you OK?" he asked from just outside the door.

"Yes," I said, surprising even myself with how cheerful I made myself sound. "I'll be out in a minute. Really. I'm fine." I did my best imitation of myself on a normal day.

"OK," he said. "If you're sure, I'm taking off. Mike's outside waiting."

"'Course, OK," I answered. "See you in a few hours?"

"Maybe," he said, his voice becoming fainter. "Depends if the bullheads are biting."

His footsteps faded, a door creaked and slammed shut. He was gone.

I began to cry, pulling the hand towel from the rack to cover my mouth with it and stifle my sobs. Finally, I stood. I splashed freezing cold water on my face, pushed in the drawer, and willed myself forward and into the living room.

"Mama, look!" Sara said, "Look what I colored!" She was lying face down on the carpet, Crayolas littering the floor around her. She had colored the Easter egg in her coloring book in bright rainbow stipes. On the facing page was a picture of a young woman wearing a fancy bonnet and carrying a basket. Her silhouette was drawn with a solid black line, one-dimensional, flat and colorless—exactly how I felt. I wished Sara would pick up a bright crayon, maybe magenta, and give her life again. If anyone could color me in, it was Sara. Instead, she tilted her head as if to say—*Why didn't Mommy gush over my picture like always?*—shrugged, and, abandoning the coloring book, she began to dance as a kazoo played the Muppet theme song.

On the coffee table, beside a few stray crayons and coloring books was the stack of Olaf's postcards I'd saved for Sara—she loved to look at the pictures. On top of the pile was a bright color photo of the Amalfi coast, wave after wave crashing against the rocky shore. Above it, the hills were ringed with narrow roads, winding higher and higher, perilously close to the cliff's edge.

Chapter Thirteen
1988-1989

June 12, 1988: The CDC reports that a new AIDS case is reported every 14 minutes.

—James Kinsella, *Covering the Plague: AIDS and the American Media*

I sat on the examining table at my general practitioner's office where he listened patiently to my complaints, my beating heart, my breathing: "Deep breath," he said. "Again." He paused to listen. "Again. Nothing unusual here, but let's get some bloodwork to be sure. CBC, metabolic panel, thyroid." He addressed this last comment to his nurse, who shuffled out, presumably to call the lab. He turned to me again. "This is how we'll do it: eliminate potential causes for your distress first. Then I'll see you back in two days—Wednesday. OK?"

The day of my follow-up appointment, I waited on the same examining table, nervously folding and unfolding the edge of the paper sheet that covered it. When I heard the clack of my chart being pulled from the plastic bin on the door, I braced myself.

"No need to sit there," Dr. Garcia said. "You may sit here," he continued, pointing to the chair beside his desk. He looked straight into my eyes. "All of your tests indicate that you are fine. Jennifer, you are a healthy young adult. Your heart, cholesterol levels, thyroid—everything checks out."

"I don't understand." I said. "But I'm so sick. I . . . I can't even go out any more. I'm missing work. I . . . my heart . . . the way it pounds, all of a sudden."

"I'm not saying there's nothing going on," he said gently. "But I believe what you are experiencing are anxiety attacks."

"*Anxiety* attacks?"

"Yes," he said. "It can be quite debilitating. Have you been under a great deal of stress?"

"Well, I guess, but . . . " I began. "No, no. That's impossible. I'm really sick. I mean, I almost passed out. The shaking . . . my heart . . . my stomach . . . "

"All signs of anxiety," he repeated.

"I . . . no," I said, indignantly. "You mean, you think I'm bringing this on myself? I'm purposely making myself sick? *Impossible.*"

Dr. Garcia's expression changed from one of a fatherly, mollifying clinician to stern parent. "Listen: I've seen this time and time again. You are not causing it, no. You are under stress. There's no shame in it. Now: I have a seriously ill man in the next room, having an EKG as we speak."

"I still can't believe this is only anxiety."

"*Only* is the wrong way to look at it. Anxiety can be incapacitating. The trick is identifying it." He took out a pad and scribbled some notes. "I'm going to refer you to a good doc, a psychologist."

"A psychologist! You think I need *therapy?*"

"A psychologist can help you understand your stressors," he said. "She'll recommend some techniques. If you commit to getting better, you will."

He handed me the note, then rushed out to his patient— the one who was actually sick.

"You'll need to complete some paperwork," said the woman, glancing at me from behind the reception desk, a phone still cradled between her ear and shoulder. Her spotless white nurse's shoes squeaked down the length of the massive intake desk as she reached for a clipboard, then handed it to me. "The doctor will be with you shortly," she added, then into the phone, "Sorry to keep you waiting. How can I help you?"

I found a seat in the waiting room and pulled the *Purdue Pharma* pen from under the clip. As instructed, I filled in my name, date, age, date of birth, and marital status on the top sheet of a survey. Then I turned the page and, under some brief written instructions, read:

> ____*I have frequent feelings of guilt.*
> ____*I have difficulty concentrating or thinking clearly.*
> ____*I have thoughts about harming myself.*
> ____*I have large gaps in memory.*
> ____*I have difficulty getting out of bed.*
> ____*I engage in voluntary vomiting.*
> ____*I have difficulty leaving my home.*

I was to assign a number to each item, 1-10, 10 being "always," 1 being "never." I flipped through the rest of the survey, six pages of similar items—everything from *I engage in inappropriate expressions of anger* to *I hear voices when no one else is present.* After the list of items were several more pages on which I was to describe in paragraph form, my current symptoms, as well as my medical history, educational background, career information, family history of addictions, and personal drug use. On the last page under a heading in bold print, *Holmes and Rahe Social Readjustment Rating Scale (SRRS)*, was a list of life experiences that psychologists had deemed stressful, and beside each, a number—the higher the number, the more stressful the event, the greater impact on individual wellbeing. I scanned the list and found *death of a close friend, major change in the health or behavior of a family member, change in workplace or responsibilities.* I set the clipboard down and waited to be called.

Dr. DeRosa wore her dark hair up, her glasses perched on the end of her straight nose. She looked at me with enormous, understanding eyes, and nodded patiently when I suggested to her that I didn't quite agree with Dr. Garcia's diagnosis and referral to her care.

"I understand your reticence. I *do,*" she said, but I could hardly concentrate on her words, so focused was I on her voice. I wondered if they taught that in shrink school, that ultra-slow, syrupy, calming tone.

"I don't want to waste your time," I said. "But I really think my problem is physical. I did the survey, but . . . all due respect . . . I don't think this is the right place for me."

I scanned the room. Everything about it confirmed my suspicions: Dr. DeRosa's prominently-displayed, mahogany-framed University of Chicago diploma; the serene pale blue walls; the distant, gentle hum of classical Muzak from the waiting room; the box of tissues set at arm's length on the end table beside me. All she needed to complete the movie-perfect-therapist image was a fainting couch.

"You *are* in the right place," Dr. DeRosa said. "And you *are* feeling sick, physically—you're right. But you can and will get better when we get to the source of your discomfort and discover what is actually bothering you."

"I hope you're right," I said, still convinced that her opening was a memorized script, like those French dialogues we had to repeat, word-for-word, in high school. "But . . . no. I don't buy that it's mental."

"Your survey responses lead me to the same conclusion drawn by Dr. Garcia," she began, "but we'll need to delve more deeply. If I'm right, you should know one thing: you have complete control over this," she said. "Even if these attacks seem completely random to you."

"So what's next?"

"Well, for today," she paused, then spoke as if her next utterance would shatter the Earth with its importance. "We just talk."

"Talk," I said, my tone laced with skepticism.

"Yes. Now, tell me under what circumstances these attacks have occurred."

"Well, mostly at work," I said. "I started a new job this year, and well, I'm a shy person deep down, and I'm feeling a little over my head."

"Say more about that," she said. "In what ways are you feeling over your head?"

"You know," I said. "I mean, these people I work with, they're so smart. Some have published books and their teaching—they just know what to do. Like, automatically."

"Well, that sounds like a great environment," she said. "You must have many good mentors."

"Oh, I do," I said. "It's just, like in meetings. I'm so afraid I'll say something stupid and make a fool of myself. You know, they'll think, like, wow—did we ever make a mistake."

Dr. DeRosa scribbled some notes on her pad. "And why would you think their hiring you was a mistake?" she asked. "You just finished telling me how smart they are. Would they not also hire a smart person like themselves?"

"I guess, I mean, I don't know. They could've messed up."

"Don't you have the qualifications for the job?" she asked. "I saw on your survey that you have a master's degree in education. Isn't that the same degree your colleagues have?"

"Yes. Well, some of them," I said. "But they're so . . . on top of it. Accomplished. Polished."

"And you are not?"

"I am not. Not like them." I thought a moment, trying to find the right words for my insecurity around my colleagues. I realized I'd begun twirling my hair and stopped myself, folding my hands in front of me. "I don't think well on my feet. I get tongue-tied. I worry they'll find out, you know . . . maybe, I'm an imposter."

"They chose you based on what you have achieved, what you have experienced. Very real qualifications. You see that, don't you?"

"I don't feel it . . . you know . . . *inside*. I'm always, well, intimidated."

"So that is stressful, especially when you are new," she said.

"Enough that I make myself sick?" I asked.

"Possibly," she said. "But let's think more broadly. Tell me: other than while at work, have you ever had the same symptoms—the racing heart, the shallow breathing, the desire to run?"

"Run? How did you . . . "

"Your survey," she said. "You mentioned that during an episode, you want to run away."

"Oh yeah, I did, didn't I? Well, let's see." I thought back. "Um, before I started working, most recently it happened when I got on a plane."

"An airplane, huh. So you have fear of flying?"

"Oh, no," I said. "I'm not afraid at all. It's being closed-in that I hate. And that I can't control the thing."

"Say more. Control what?"

"You know, the plane," I said. "That's why I like driving myself. I don't like being a passenger. Especially in the back seat. I always think: If I drive, I can stop and get out whenever I want. When I feel trapped—even thinking about it, I start sweating."

"The back seat," she said. "Did you ever have a bad experience there, in a back seat?"

"No . . . I don't think so . . . " I began. Then, I remembered. "Wait—yeah, come to think of it. Me and Mom and Dad—we got in a terrible accident when I was in high school. Dad was driving. I was in the back seat—kinda trapped in there till the ambulance arrived."

"That kind of trauma sticks with a person," she said. "How could it not have affected you?"

"I guess. I never thought of that."

"But, getting back to the plane," she said. "Now, you said you had this anxiety attack recently on a plane?"

"Yes, well," I began. "Really, even before I got on the plane. Like from the moment I woke up that morning, I was sick to my stomach. Just dreading the whole thing."

"And where were you going?"

"I was . . . I went to Chicago. A funeral."

"A funeral," she said. "That is stressful in itself, no? And with whom did you travel?"

"Oh, alone," I said, forcing a matter-of-fact tone. "I went alone. To meet my brother. My husband had to stay back—you know, to care for our kids."

"So you were alone on this plane," she began.

"It . . . um . . . " I tried to speak, but, without warning, I began to cry.

"It's OK," she said soothingly. "Death of a friend or relative—-most of us cry when we are reminded unexpectedly."

I pulled a tissue from the dispenser that had been conveniently placed on the table beside me. I tried desperately to suppress my tears, and behind them, the anger that welled up and through them. I'd had enough with her probing questions. I was done. I stiffened, sat straight in the chair, and forced my sobs back down where they belonged.

"Perhaps we talk more about the funeral at our next session?" Dr. DeRosa asked, straightening herself, her tone becoming suddenly more businesslike, suggesting closure. *Had she looked at her watch or just noticed my body language?* "But make no mistake," she continued. "What you are experiencing is very real. A *physiological* reality. It is called the 'fight or flight' response—I'm sure you remember it from your psychology classes."

"I do, yes."

"Here is what happens to you: the insecurity that you carry is triggered by stimuli with which you already associate negatively—a claustrophobic airplane seat, an encounter where you feel singled-out or trapped. And when that happens, you feel a surge of adrenaline and an overpowering need to escape the situation. But the situation is merely the trigger. It isn't the meeting or the airplane that you are truly running from. You understand?"

"Yes. I get it," I said. "But it's so horrible. I actually thought I was dying the last time. Like it might be a stroke or something."

"I know. That's what I'm telling you. You are not imagining it: it is a very real physical outcome of what stress is doing to your body."

"At least it's a biological thing," I said. "Like I'm not crazy, making it happen."

"The important thing now is *you know what it is*. And I can assure you: it will not kill you. Now, when you feel it coming on, you can tell yourself: Oh, this again. I know what this is."

"But . . . what do I do?"

"You can train yourself to change your response. You can actually stop the attack by regulating your breathing. Just practice this exercise over and over: take a very deep breath."

"You mean now?"

Yes, now. Try it."

I breathed deeply, or so I thought.

"Deeper," she said. "A long, slow breath, so deep your belly expands. Try again."

I breathed deeply.

"Deeper. Extend your belly. Yes, that's it. Now: let the air out gradually, as slowly as you possibly can. That's it. Count, slowly: 1001, 1002, 1003—all the way to 1008."

"This? This will control my anxiety attacks?" I asked, still skeptical.

"Yes," she said. "I know it sounds implausible given what you've experienced. And I won't lie to you: it is difficult in the moment of extreme panic to do it. But if you practice, you'll see, it's simple physiology. The controlled breathing slows everything down. Again. Try again."

I breathed in deeply, counted it out slowly, with a bit more success.

"Good!" she said. "Your heart will gradually stop racing, your concentration will return." She handed me a book, *Anxiety and Panic Attacks: Their Cause and Cure*, and continued. "Here: read this. It describes some other techniques too—like visualization. Read this section carefully. You can find something simple—a place or an experience with which you associate positively. You can conjure it in your mind, reimagining your environment in the moment. It can be a very powerful tool, visualization. For now, practice, practice, practice. Then come and see me next week. In the meantime, I'm going to call Dr. Garcia and ask him to give you a script for some Xanax." Responding to me look of alarm, she added, "Very low dose. Don't worry."

"I'll try," I said. "Thanks, Dr. DeRosa."

I left the office, appointment card in hand.

On the street, the April snowbanks melted, one drop at a time, turning them to dirt-encrusted mounds, tiny tributaries trickling from their edges into street grates and curb-side puddles. Like their gradual waning, the heaviness in my chest dissipated ever so slightly that day. I walked to the car feeling a bit lighter, turned the key in the ignition, and sat a moment before putting the car in reverse. I breathed in, held the air deep inside, then counted out my exhale: one-thousand-one, one-thousand-two . . .

I talked myself into going back to work. I got through one day, then the next. Still my dread grew as the date of the next faculty meeting approached. I'd practiced the breathing exercises and worked on visualization with Dr. DeRosa at weekly appointments, so—braced, but determined—when the meeting day came, I sat toward the back of the auditorium, silently counting out my exhales. When the College President began to call on departments for updates, I stiffened. In the midst of a long, protracted exhale, I mentally reenacted the self-talk I had rehearsed: *Visualize the place you have felt most free,* and repeated the mantra, *You are back at Loon Lake. You are back at Loon Lake. On the raft. You're safe, next to Olaf.* Slowly, I let myself drift into memory:

The fluffy clouds above us, spun like the cotton candy at the midway, stretch and turn, forming tails and noses and ears. Olaf and I lie on the weathered wooden raft and watch as the clouds twist into animals with enormous eyes and ears, then elongate into men with canes, one with a top hat. The clouds cannot hide the determined sun that warms my skin, drying the dots of water left on my legs and arms from wading through the lake that surrounds us. Olaf says he sees a giant hippo next to a skinny giraffe, and then I can see them too, these animals that don't exist until my brother names them. We watch until the hippo's head widens here and shrinks there, becoming a row of ducklings, missing only their mother duck. I dangle my hand over the side of the raft, letting the cool lake water filter through my fingers. The dock sways softly with the rhythm of the water beneath us, rocking us gently till we doze in the afternoon heat, side-by-side.

"Anything else for the good of the order?" the President bellowed from his podium, shaking me from my daydream. The faculty considered each other gravely, as if to say, *Don't even dare.* "All right, then. Adjourned!" he boomed. And with those words, I realized I had not merely survived the faculty meeting; I had done so with the help of Dr. DeRosa—and memories of Olaf.

"Oh, man, Holine," Olaf said. "This is heaven." He was finally home for a week before heading back to Italy for the second summer in a row. He took a sip of his iced tea from a bendy straw; the ice tinkled in his glass. Olaf and I reclined, side-by-side, in woven yellow lounge chairs beside our backyard pool, soaking up the rays. The July sun baked our skin through a film of coconut sunscreen, releasing that delicious summer scent, one I always associated with our lazy vacation days.

"Just like when we were kids, right? On the roof outside your window!" I said. "I've been waiting for this all year."

"How great is it that we both have summers off?" he said, spritzing himself with cool water from a spray bottle.

"This ten-month gig is the best," I said.

"So, no more troubles?" he asked, "I mean, your work anxiety stuff?"

"So much better," I said. "I've been seeing my shrink-lady for only a few months, and I have to admit it: she had me down from day one."

"Yeah, anxiety is a bitch," he said. "You and me and Dad."

"I knew about you...but, *Dad?*"

"*Yeah*, Dad. I thought you knew.

"I guess I just didn't put it together," I said. "Like, when? I mean, with you it was obvious. Every single time in church, you wouldn't just get pale, you'd be—I mean, *chalky* white, like in a second. I just thought you were scared of going to hell or something."

"Ha!" he said. "Maybe so. But Dad—he was another story."

"He actually got sick?"

"Oh, yeah. You were pretty little when it started," he began. "Too young to catch on, I guess...but remember? Every time he had to travel, he'd get so sick. Remember that time? Him canceling his work trip?"

"That's right. I remember now: Dad sitting at the kitchen bar, stewing every time he had to go on a business trip. His face—he was so *uncomfortable*—so conflicted. I just never knew what it was. Dumb kid—what did I know?"

"Yup. Every time. Poor Dad."

"If only we could get him to counseling, so he'd know what I know now . . . but, yeah, like he's gonna see a shrink."

"Never happen."

"If he knew how much it helps, he'd go," I said. "I can't even explain how sick I felt. I probably sound like a drama queen, but I was sure I was dying."

"I never had it as bad as you," he said. "Probably 'cuz I'd just bolt. But I do remember the feeling. It's pretty devastating for the few moments when you feel stuck, like you can't get out."

"Like being in an elevator, the doors closed *forever*. It's always there, a constant battle."

"Well, I think you're brave," Olaf said. "Lots of people would've stayed in the house forever than risk feeling that way again."

"And, speaking of brave," I said, "you're off to Europe again in a week! You're the one with some guts—flying all that way with only a backpack and a rail pass. I would be freaked."

"It doesn't seem brave to me at all," he said. "Just another adventure. It's just so—it's a different world. Kind of a charmed, yet grungy existence all at once. It's elegant and historical and old world all mixed up with our modern mess. I just love it so much!"

"And you get to practice your Italian," I said.

"With *real* Italians," he said, "The language is so beautiful—nothing like that ugly dialect Gramma used to speak."

"No doubt it's great practice," I said. "But, you know I worry." Olaf gave me his *not this again* look. "I know, but are you sure you're up to it? I mean, you just got out for the summer, you just finished directing the choral piece. Don't you ever rest?"

"I'm fine," he said. He sat up straight, looked me in the eye. "I'm *fine.*"

"OK, OK," I said. "But . . . I . . . I gotta ask something…"

"So?"

"Well," I began. "There's a test now, a more reliable one. Have you considered it?"

"'Course," he said. "I mean, I've thought about it. But no. No test for me."

"I understand, I do," I said. "It's horribly scary. But still, *imagine!* If you're negative, no more worry. And if you got bad news, there's a chance now, you know, there are new drugs."

"'Course I know that." He thought a minute. "But . . . people I know taking stuff . . . it's toxic. I see my friends poisoning themselves for an extra month or two of misery. Besides, in a way, it's riskier. Getting tested."

"Yeah, I remember you saying how a positive test can be used against people."

"You don't know what it's like, *really* like, out there," he said. "The stigma. People are losing their jobs. And then there's the rumors—about camps." He lowered his voice to a hush, "Camps . . . it's awful."

"*Camps?*"

"They hate us, *hate* us," he said, casting his angry eyes downward.

"Who? You mean—the government?"

"*Yes,* the government. People are actually afraid they'll put us in camps. Quarantine the positive cases. You know this, right? The only reason they finally developed a test at all? It's to protect the blood supply—to test the people donating. Now that they have it, who knows how that information could be used."

"But . . . " I looked at him, confused.

"Don't you get it?" he asked, exasperated. "*We're* the enemy. Not the virus. My friends, my Teddy. Surely you've heard what they're saying. Reagan's own communications director—that idiot Buchanan—said it out loud *and* in print:

AIDS is 'nature's revenge on gay men.'" Olaf sat straight up in the lounger, slid his feet to the side to face me, his face reddening. The floodgates had opened, and the worries from which he might normally have protected me came spilling out .

"Yeah, I heard that. I was hoping you hadn't. He's so hateful."

"*Gay plague*, they used to call it," he said, shaking his head angrily. "Like the first ones to get it—a *virus!*—are the cause of it. It's genocide, plain and simple. Intentional neglect, that's what's killing us!"

"I know, honey," I said, reaching for his hand. "I'm so sorry. I didn't mean to upset you."

"They actually make jokes about it," he said. "They joked about sending Qaddafi to San Francisco so he would get it. Reagan himself. And the Secretary of State."

"What?" I said. "No!—I knew they were horrible, but . . . ."

"And what about that Pat Robertson?" he asked.

"The 700-Club guy?"

"Yeah. *Him*. People listen to that bullshit *every day. Every day*. While my friends are dying, Pat Robertson is parroting Jerry Falwell and their *Moral Majority*. Yeah, moral: letting people die."

"Oh, Olaf . . ."

"It's not just Reagan—that coward, never even *saying* 'AIDS' in public until his buddy Rock Hudson died. And Bush has been—just more of the same. Sure, easy for them to dismiss us, but out in the real world—it's *scary* out there."

"What do you mean?"

"The hate they spew on TV," he said. "It ends up in the streets. You wouldn't believe how these vile people roam the streets—all our neighborhoods and hangouts—just looking for gay people to beat up. My friends and I . . . we've started to watch where we walk at night. Making sure we're home early, never walking alone—all that."

"You're *serious?*"

"Read the news," he said. "That is . . . when they bother to actually cover it. Attacks on gay men are out of control. I mean it. Look it up. Where is the message about keeping us safe? Where is the protection?"

"Oh my God," I shook my head in disbelief.

"What can we do? All we can do is take care of ourselves, as best we can. Be vigilant. No one else will care for us."

"I will," I said. I looked deeply in his eyes. "No. I will. I *mean* it."

"I know," he said, smiling weakly. "I'm sorry, Holine. I shouldn't lay all this on you. It's just, sometimes, I get so angry."

"Of course you do," I said. "How could you not be enraged? The entire country should be enraged!"

"Let's just . . . Let's just try to enjoy the day. C'mon." He adjusted the back of the lounger to its lowest position, then handed me the spray bottle. "Now, wouldja spray some of that cool water on my back? It's getting toasty out here. Let's talk about something grand! I know! My upcoming trip to Italy!"

He rolled over on the chaise, and, as he did, the waistband of his shorts slipped downward, ever so slightly. There, above the edge, raised above his skin, I saw it. Gaping. Raw. The outline of a large mulberry spot.

A spot.

Exactly the size of my balled fist.

Chapter Fourteen
1993

Only an eternal optimist would have left the ninth international AIDS meeting here last week believing that new drugs will be available anytime soon to save the lives of the 14 million people now infected with the virus that causes AIDS. Or believing that a vaccine would be developed in time to prevent the number of those infected from soaring to at least 30 million by the year 2000, as the World Health Organization predicts.

—Lawrence K. Altman, Conference Ends with Little Hope for AIDS Cure, *The New York Times*

Two a.m.

A faint sliver of light from a nearby streetlight filtered through the curtains. Otherwise, the kitchen was deathly dark.

A few minutes earlier—or maybe it was a half hour?—I'd wrenched myself out of my twisted sheets and tiptoed to the kitchen, as far as possible from the kids' bedrooms. I had no idea what to do once I got there. I leaned against the cupboard and slid down to the floor, burying my face in my hands to muffle the sound.

It is hard to cry quietly.

All night I'd wrestled with myself about what I had to face the next day. I would tell my father what my mother couldn't bear to say, what she'd left me to say instead. She had put off the conversation ever since she found out, every day for months, and now, all the time we'd had, all the opportunities, had dwindled to just one day. Only one day before Paul and I would board a plane for Atlanta to pick up Olaf.

It was easy to assemble the words.

Dad, Olaf has AIDS. He is very sick and needs our help. He is extremely weak; sometimes, he is confused. His illness has progressed to the point that he cannot live alone. He will be here tomorrow, and he'll stay with you and Mom. I've known about his illness for a while. In fact, I've known he was gay since I was 17. I'm sorry I never told you, but that story was not mine to tell.

Finding the words was not difficult. The difficulty was getting myself to speak them aloud. The difficulty was knowing the anguish my words would cause. The difficulty was realizing that, as soon as the words were spoken, I'd want to rage and scream, to pull the words from the air before Dad could hear them, to erase them from memory, to make them not merely untrue, but unthinkable. To keep Dad safe in the protective web of denial he'd spun around himself. To wrap Dad in my arms, to dry his tears forever.

My stomach churned. I grabbed the edge of the trash can and slid it beside me, just in case.

Time and again, the memory resurfaced of that June day Olaf and I had talked by the pool, and what I'd seen, tucked beneath his waistband. In the days that followed, it diminished in my consciousness, as I willed it from a manifestation of disease to just another ugly bruise. *Hadn't I gotten huge purplish contusions from God-knows-where?* But then another smaller blemish had appeared while he drifted across Italy that July. By the time he'd returned from Europe for his end-of-summer visit, the new spot on his forehead had faded, barely visible beneath the shiny, longer hair that fell across his forehead, barely grazing his eyebrows. I dismissed it as a sunspot from all that outdoor exposure in the blazing Italian heat. He seemed OK—thinner, maybe, his cheekbones more prominent. But he talked excitedly about the upcoming school year, just like always, and days after arriving back home that August, he began teaching. Nothing had changed.

Then, mid-school-year, on an unremarkable Monday evening after a typical day—the kind of day that is subsumed into weeks and months of sameness, never to be remembered—the phone rang. Sara, done with her third-grade social studies worksheet, practiced *The Spinning Song* on the piano, her tiny fingers flying impatiently across the keys as she raced to the finish, skimming over notes in the process. Down the hall in his room, Paul Joe, his head bent in frustration over his six-grade math homework, fretted at his desk, furiously erasing computations. In the kitchen, I rinsed the dinner dishes and stacked them in the dishwasher. I hadn't checked the caller ID when the phone rang, just snapped it up quickly so that the kids wouldn't race to get it, the ringing phone a handy excuse to abandon their tasks.

"Holine," Olaf had said quietly, more a statement than a greeting, almost as if he'd hoped I wouldn't answer.

"Olaf!" I said, turning off the water, so I could hear. "What's up?"

"I . . . um," he began. There was an unnatural quality about his voice—it was higher, more tentative. He paused for several moments.

"Sara!" I yelled, covering the mouthpiece to spare Olaf my screeching. "Stop banging the keys!" Then, into the phone, "Sorry—so, what's up? You OK?"

"That's just it," he said. "Why I'm calling. The test . . . my results came back." He hesitated again.

I sank to the floor.

"No."

"I knew it," he said. "Let's face it: we both knew it."

I couldn't speak, couldn't catch my breath.

"Holine? I'm sorry . . . "

"I . . . oh, no," I said. "I can't . . . "

"Listen, Holine," he said. "I'm so sorry. It's my own . . . if only I'd . . . "

"No!" I cried. "Don't do that. Don't *ever* do that. It's not your fault. It's a virus. It could've happened to any of us."

"But, if I'd known . . . " he began. "You have to know, I hate how this hurts you."

"Nobody knew. *Nobody*," I said. "Listen, just don't worry about me. You're what's important here. I mean, what does the doctor say?"

"Dr. Goodson," he said. "You remember? She took care of Teddy. She said there are new drug combinations—AZT and some other stuff, D-something-or-other. If it works, it'll keep the virus from replicating. That is, if the damn drugs don't kill me first."

"Don't say that!"

"No, really, she's on top of it," he said. "Seriously, Holine. I couldn't be in better hands."

"What else? What else did she say?"

"Just . . . she's not happy with my T-cell count," he said.

"T-cell count?"

"Yeah, T-cells, the ones that fight off infections and diseases—I don't have enough," he said. "Probably, I'll have to have a transfusion. But she said it'll give me a little more pep."

"A *transfusion*? I hate to think of you going through this," I said. "I can come if . . . "

"Stop," he said. "You've got your hands full. Rayanne'll come keep me company. And, really, I'm doing well, despite it all. I'm *bone*-tired—and you know—my stomach's a mess. But right now, no fever. I'm no worse than before we knew—still working, going strong."

"It's just—now it's real." My voice faded to a whisper.

"I know," he said, the words catching in his throat. "Seeing that diagnosis in black and white on her prescription pad . . . " Then, seeming to collect himself, he said firmly, "Listen. Please. Try not to worry. The only thing that's changed is . . . now we know. And, in a way, maybe it's good. Now, at least I'll have the medicine. I have the best care."

"What can I do?" I asked, desperately. "I need to help. Is there anything?"

"What can anyone do, really?" he responded. "There's nothing."

"Call me? You *have* to swear, you'll call me if you need me."

"I'll call you," he said. "And I'll call even when I don't need you. I promise."

"Don't try to spare me," I said. "I *mean* it. I need to know what's happening."

"I know," he said. "I love you, Holine. I'll call you soon. Promise."

"OK. I love you, too."

I waited to hear the click of his receiver before I could bring myself to hang up.

I burrowed into the corner of the kitchen peninsula, my face pressed into my knees to mute the sobs rising from a place so deep, as though a chasm had opened up within me, plumbing downward into a bottomless howl of grief. I could not move; I could no longer trust my legs to support me. As the minutes passed, I was unaware of Sara, still plunking away on the piano—that is, until it was suddenly silent.

The kids. What if they had they heard?

I forced myself up and forward in their direction. In the living room, Sara turned the page of her music book and began tracing her fingers up and down the D major scale. Her piano-playing had given me cover. At his desk, Paul Joe frowned into his math book. I walked into my bathroom and shut the door, ran the cold water over a washcloth, wrung it weakly, and held it against one eye, then the other. When I pulled away the dripping cloth, I was unsettled by my reflection—not by my slightly puffy eyes, but because, physically, I appeared unchanged. It seemed impossible. I was no longer the same person.

From the living room, I heard an announcer hawking something on the TV. Sara, done practicing, had turned on her favorite show promptly at eight o'clock, following the rules: practice for a half hour; get a half hour of TV. The next moment, I heard Will Smith's familiar rap: "Now this is the story all about how my life got flipped, turned upside-down . . . "

True to his word, after that night, Olaf called more often. He pushed on through exhaustion-filled days, continuing to teach high school. In the evenings, he was out almost every night, unwilling to relinquish his sessions with a language coach, his Thursday night choir practice, or his Sunday choir gig. Returning to the apartment, he plummeted into sleep, free-falling into a fitful slumber, restless with feverish dreams, his morning sheets damp with sweat. The next day, he powered through again, summoning a strength that belied his five-foot-seven, 130-pound frame, through sheer force of will. Defying time, determined to outrun it.

My new caller ID lit up, flashing Olaf's familiar number, red digits parading across a tiny rectangular screen. I picked up, surprising him not with "hello," but with a cherry, "Olaf! It's you!"

"Holine," he tried to continue but burst into tears.

"Olaf! What is it?"

"I'm . . . " he choked. "I have to stop," he sobbed. "Teaching! I have to quit teaching."

"Oh no," I said. "I'm so sorry! Oh, Olaf!" He tried to speak, but could not, his sobs overtaking him. "So . . . " I began, swallowing the lump in my throat, "So, you just take a leave, right? Maybe it's temporary. Just a setback."

"No, no," he moaned. "Retirement," he managed to utter through his tears. "I'm 41-years old, and I have to retire."

"But . . . "

"No, Holine," he said firmly. "I can't do it anymore."

"Oh, no. How is this even happening?"

"And the kids!" he said. "They had this program, you know, this 'Teacher of the Year' thing. All my kids in the auditorium. They gave me this plastic trophy and a framed picture of the class—you know, the Italian III kids, the ones I took to Italy. They *sang* to me in Italian! I just wept. And, oh, Holine! They were all crying."

"They love you," I said, now sobbing along with him.

"But . . . I just can't. I can't," he said. "Only one month to go, and I can't even make it to the end of the school year. If I keep up like this, it'll kill me. It's all just too much."

"I know, Honey. I know," I said. "Come home! Please—can't you come home for a while?"

"I will," he said. "Just as soon as I've gotten a little rest. I will."

Olaf somehow ventured off on his annual trip to Italy. However, this time, no post cards. No letters. Radio silence. When he returned, although he called often, he barely spoke about the trip. He became more distant, evasive. I'd ask what he was doing, if he was keeping his appointments and taking his medicine. His answers were general; his sentences clipped: he was hanging out with friends; he was taking the medicine even though it made him weak and achy and exhausted. He slept a lot. He read books. Then he slept some more.

Each day before bed, Sara drew an "X" on the calendar, counting down the days before our annual end-of-summer trip to Yankee Stadium. For me, each "X" marked another summer day that had passed without a visit from Olaf. For many weeks. I had held out hope that one day the phone would ring and Olaf would say he was on his way. But by the time we packed our bags and cooler in the trunk and headed east toward the city, my hopes dissolved with the waning daylight. It had become clear that Olaf was not going to visit.

The kids and I hit the stores for back-to-school shopping, our annual ritual. We wandered down aisles packed with cellophaned number two pencils, lined pads and Trapper Keepers, rulers and black-speckled composition books, filling our shopping cart with folders, notebooks, crayons and pens. At Bradlees, Sara chose an Aladdin lunchbox, and Paul Joe picked out a camo backpack. At the mall, we bought Sara print pants with matching scrunchies at the Children's Place, Gap khakis and golf shirts for Paul Joe. Then, the mad dash began: the kids' bus at 8:30, me tearing into the college parking lot by 9:00, all of us enmeshed in our relentless, frenetic routine, every day the same.

One afternoon, the caller ID flashed an unknown number.

"Jennifer?" a voice asked, uncertainly. "Is this Jennifer? Holine?"

"Yes," I said tentatively, thrown off by the nickname only Olaf called me.

"Hi, it's Mike. You know—your brother's friend?"

"Oh yeah," I said. "Mike. Everything alright?"

"Well," he began. "That's why I'm calling. Your brother—he's having a rough time."

"What? What do you mean? What's happening?" For a moment it seemed my heart had actually stopped beating.

"He's gotten worse," he said. "His stomach, fever." I felt for the stool behind me, and sat. *Oh no, no, no.* "He didn't tell me. How...?"

"He's so weak," he said. "Rayanne took him to the doctor yesterday, and to tell the truth, I'm surprised they didn't admit him."

"Oh, God. No."

"Listen, he's . . . " he hesitated. "He needs help. He shouldn't be alone."

"It's that bad? Oh, oh, no," I cried. "Of course. I can come, or . . . "

"We tried, you know," he said. "Me. Rayanne. One of us has been there every day. But we have to work, and honestly, it's gotten to that point. Even if we weren't working, he needs more than we can manage."

"How . . . how bad is it?" The words caught in my throat.

"*Bad.*"

"I knew it was coming, but I just . . . I thought we had more time."

"We're out of time," Mike said. "You need to come here, or he needs to be there."

"OK. I'll . . . I'll figure something out."

"There's more," Mike said, haltingly. "He's started to do things—things that don't make sense. We find clothes in the refrigerator, plates in the trash. For days he lost the portable phone. He can't be without a phone."

"Oh no. Oh my God."

"Not all the time, you know, but he gets confused. I'm afraid he's going to hurt himself," Mike said.

"What do you mean?" I asked, horrified.

"Not intentionally, no. I just mean that sometimes he's just not thinking straight. It comes and goes. The other day I stopped by, and he'd fallen asleep on the couch. There was just . . . just *stuff* everywhere—shoes, notebooks, albums out of jackets, mail, receipts—just scattered. The TV was on, like way too loud, and food—I can't tell you what it was—burning on the stove. If I hadn't gotten there . . . "

"No." I started to cry.

"I know," he said. "I'm so sorry to have to tell you all this. But it's important that you know. And more important that he gets some help."

"I'll, uh . . . " I thought a moment. "Give me a couple days. I have to find him a doctor here. Talk with my parents. I'll get back to you."

"Soon," Mike said.

"Soon."

That night as soon as Paul got home from work, I rushed to the door and threw my arms around him.

190

"It's Olaf!" I began to cry the second I spoke the words. "He's worse. Somehow, we need to get him home."

"What happened?"

"Mike called," I said. "It's to the point . . . it's bad . . . Mike and Rayanne—they're afraid to leave him alone." Paul lowered himself into a kitchen chair, his eyes filling with tears. "I don't know how to do this. I'm not sure—is it safe for him to fly alone? In his state of mind? With his weakness?"

"He's *that* sick?"

"Yes, and Mike said he gets confused sometimes—really confused," I said. "Paul, he fell asleep while food was burning on the stove."

"Oh, Jen . . . no."

"We have to *do* something."

"I'm so sorry," he said. Paul pulled a handkerchief from his pocket and handed it to me.

"Now, listen . . . " Paul began. He took both my hands in his and looked me straight in the eyes. "Here's an idea: we just fly there and bring him back," he said, as if it was the most logical thing in the world, flying three hours to escort a 41-year-old man to his plane and accompany him back the way we'd come.

"But how? How do we explain it? Won't he feel like we're kidnapping him?"

"We make it seem like he needs a little vacation. You know," he said. "Everyone misses him, he's not working . . . why not come visit?"

"Vacation? You think he'll buy that?"

"And his birthday—it's next week, right?" Paul asked.

"Yes, actually—it is."

"So you tell him, you know, like, 'Surprise! Guess who's coming to Atlanta for your birthday!'" he said. "He won't fight you. He'd never hurt your feelings."

"I guess. It might just work."

"Besides," he added. "Deep down, don't you think he knows he needs us now? I think he'll be relieved."

"Well, we have to do something," I said. "OK. Lemme call Mom before I lose my nerve."

"Oh, jeez, Jen," Paul looked at me with eyes that reflected my own dread.

"I know," I said. "I gotta get it over with."

I retreated to the bedroom, shut the door. I sunk to the floor, whispered a silent prayer, picked up the portable, and dialed Mom's number.

"Mom," I said. "You alone?"

"Yeah," she said. "Just getting supper on the table."

"I, uh, just got off the phone," I said. "It's Olaf. He's worse, Mom. He needs to come home." For several moments, she said nothing. "Mom, you there?"

"What happened?" she asked, her voice shaking.

"Mike called," I said. "It's not good. He has new symptoms, scary ones."

" Scary? What do you mean, scary?" Mom gasped.

"He needs us now. It's gotten to the point that he shouldn't be alone."

Mom drew in her breath, seeming to stifle a sob.

"No, Jen," she said. "Tell me this isn't happening."

"I wish I could, Mom," I said. "But, it's time. It's all settled. Paul and I are going to get him."

"But how?"

"I'm booking our flights," I said. "Soon as we can, we're going."

"But," she began. "He—he'll need a doctor."

"I know people—the AIDS Coalition. They'll know who to call. I'll do it tomorrow."

"But . . . " she began to cry. "Oh . . . what are we going to do? What are we going to do?"

"We'll do what we have to."

"If only we had more time. . ." she choked between sobs, her words drifting off.

"I'm so sorry, Mom. But time's up, and this means . . . " I began. "You know what this means: we have to tell Dad."

"Oh, God," she said, sobbing. "I can't. How can I tell him this? I can't. Not this."

"I'll do it then," I said. "I'll tell him. Tomorrow."

Two-forty a.m.

My back still pressed against a kitchen cabinet and no closer to knowing how to break it to Dad, I began to pray. *God, please help us. God, please, please help us. My father. My father. Our father. Our Father, who art in heaven . . . Our Father, who art in heaven, our father, our father . . .* I prayed and prayed. The kitchen clock marked the seconds, *tick, tick, tick . . .*

On the cold linoleum, I curled into myself, pulling my knees to my chest, rocking back and forth, praying and rocking, praying and rocking. Then, a whisper that I realized was my own voice: *Our Father. My father. He will understand.*

The next day when I arrived at Mom and Dad's, Mom met me in the doorway, her usually made-up face pale, twisted into the saddest expression I'd ever seen. "I told him," she said flatly. "I told him myself."

I found Dad in the den, slumped forward in his recliner, weeping, one hand shading his eyes. I said nothing, just reached out and hugged him as he cried, silent tears coursing down his cheeks. We stayed that way, wrapped in each other's arms for the better part of the afternoon.

Chapter Fifteen
1993

When I walk down Castro Street, I know that this is where Bill died, this is where Henry died. This is where George committed suicide after his diagnosis. This is the building from which Freddie was evicted when his landlord found out.

—Cleve Jones, speech, University of Maryland

When the alarm rang at 5:30 the next morning, I was already bracing for a day of marathon travel: Paul maneuvering the car through rush hour traffic to Syracuse, followed by flights from Syracuse to New York, New York to Atlanta, taxi to Olaf's, only to turn around and do it all in reverse. Grueling as the journey might be, the acidic churn in my stomach had more to do with how we might find Olaf: packed, bright-eyed and ready, or confused and disheveled. Or worse: ill and diminished, maybe forgetting our plan entirely.

When we arrived at Olaf's apartment, we found him ready and waiting, sagging under an oversized parka too bulky to pack. Looking fragile and faded, his vacant eyes, rimmed in black, stood out against the pale skin of his face. He didn't rise to hug me as he usually would have. Instead, he mumbled an incomprehensible greeting and rose slowly, steadying himself against the arm of the couch. Beside him was one small carry-on, a mixed signal indeed: he'd armed himself against the approaching New York winter but packed for a long weekend. He bent to reach for the handle, but Paul got to it first.

"It's OK. I got you," Paul said softly.

On the plane ride home, Olaf was subdued, detached and contemplative, alternately shivering and zoning out. Lost in his huge coat, he seemed to shrink further inside it, withering before our eyes. Every so often, he muttered to himself, picking furiously at the fabric of his parka as though to remove some invisible pest. Alarmed, I stared down at the muddy edge of my boots as if concentrating on a tangible object could break these transitory visions. By the time we reached Mom and Dad's house, Olaf barely managed a few hugs before he dropped onto the fold-out couch.

After a fitful night's sleep, I returned to Mom and Dad's house early the next morning, my Dodge Shadow rattling to a stop on the side-street. I turned off the ignition and sat for a minute, messing with my school bag, pretending to search for something in case someone was looking out the window. I swallowed hard, pulled down the visor and flipped open the mirror, examining my eyes for signs of the puffiness I'd tried to cover with drugstore make-up. Fishing in my purse, I pulled a plastic bottle from the bottom and gave each eye a squirt of Visine. After one last look in the mirror, I slung the bag on my shoulder, stepped out of the car, and walked to the back door of Mom's house.

The kitchen smelled of fresh coffee, toast, and green peppers sauteed into a mostly-untouched omelet. It was placed on an ornate platter—one of Mom's "good" dishes—in the center of the breakfast table. Olaf sat beside Dad, a half-drunk cup of coffee on the table in his "World's Best Grandpa" mug. Olaf picked at his bowl of corn flakes while he read the back of the cereal box. Spread in front of Dad was a row of prescription bottles. Dad picked up a bottle, considered it closely, then drew a line and made a notation on a piece of paper in front of him.

"Hey, Jen," Dad said, proudly surveying his project. "Look—I'm making a schedule to keep track of all these meds."

Just then, Mom walked in the room, all made-up, dressed and ready for our trip to Syracuse. She took one look at Olaf and Dad and the chart before him, then at me. A single tear rolled down her cheek as she stepped slowly backwards, then turned down the hall and ducked back into the bathroom. I swallowed the sob that caught in my throat, and sat next to Olaf.

"Ready in a flash," he said. Then, studying me more closely, he added, "It's OK, Holine."

"You ride up front with Jen," Mom said to Olaf, who'd begun to protest. "Please—you'll be more comfy," she said, then scooted into the back seat behind me. She passed a lap blanket over the seatback. "Here, Jen—cover his legs." When Olaf was buckled and tucked in beside me, I let the car run a minute, then headed toward the boulevard, finally turning west onto the New York State Thruway, toward Syracuse. Snow fell lightly and was just beginning to accumulate, leaving the road shrouded in white.

"Snow," Olaf said. "Already." His enormous down-filled coat practically swallowed him up, his tiny frame shivering within it.

"I'm sorry," I said. "This tin can takes forever to warm up."

He looked out the windshield into the distance, and as I glanced over, he looked back at me, resignation washing over his face, and then . . . nothing. For a moment, he stared vacantly toward me, as if he wasn't actually seeing me. Then, jumping as if startled, he peered down at his sleeve and he began to pick at it, pulling and pulling at nothing, as if his coat was crawling with bugs or covered in lint. I looked closely at his sleeve. No bugs. No lint. Nothing.

"Huh. I can't seem to . . . " he began.

"What's wrong?" I asked.

He looked my way, but again, his eyes didn't register. "Oh, Rayanne . . . just . . . it's nothing." He stared down at his sleeve, and becoming visibly distressed, began again, furiously picking and pulling at it—at the shoulder, the elbow, the wristband.

"You OK, O.?" I asked. I eased off the gas, ready to pull over.

He looked my way again, then suddenly seemed to come back from wherever he was. "Oh! Holine!" he said, as if surprised to see me. "Sheesh, Holine. If you're gonna be my designated driver, can't we—I don't know—stop off for a cocktail or something?" he laughed.

After that, he was silent, as if he recognized that something had occurred, that he'd done something unusual—or seen something that no one else had seen. He shut his eyes and dozed the rest of the way, right up until I stopped to retrieve the parking ticket outside SUNY Health Science Center.

Inside, Olaf was immediately admitted, then swiftly tucked into a wheelchair and spirited down a hallway by a cheerful, fresh-faced young man. Mom and I settled in a waiting room with matching blue love seats and a recliner that faced a TV hanging from metal brackets, Erica Kane of *All My Children* sashaying from one end of the screen to the other. The walls were covered with flowered wallpaper, a repeating pattern of burgundy hearts forming the border that edged the ceiling—the hospital's attempt to make homey a room that felt anything but. Mom stared at the TV, clutching and not drinking the cup of lukewarm coffee given to her by a thoughtful nurse's aide. I pulled a folder from my bag and, centering my *English for Non-Native Speakers* text as a makeshift desk on my lap, tried to focus my attention on a pile of essays I should've graded a week earlier.

After what seemed an eternity, a man poked his head in the room, introducing himself as Dr. Daly, the Health-Science Center's foremost HIV specialist.

"Could you girls come this way?"

We leapt up, following him down a hall to a narrow conference room. He motioned us into seats across from him. Already at the table, there was a woman dressed not in a uniform or doctor's coat, but plain-clothed, like us, a nametag pinned to her lapel.

"You're his mother?" the doctor directed the question toward Mom.

"Yes—is everything alright? Where's my son?"

"This is Beth Jones, our social worker." The doctor motioned to the woman, who half-stood and reached out her hand to shake mine.

"Good to meet you," I said, weakly shaking Beth's hand. Mom nodded in her direction.

"Now, I'm sorry to tell you," Dr. Daly said resolutely. "But your son is very seriously ill. He has advanced cancer of the liver. At this point, impossible to treat."

Mom grabbed the edge of the table to steady herself. "Liver cancer? How?"

"This is what often happens," he explained. "This disease compromises the immune system, allowing any number of infections, even cancers, to proliferate." He took a breath, then continued. "I'm so sorry I don't have better news."

Mom stared at Dr. Daly, at first unable to process, then urgently sought Beth's eyes, hoping for clarification.

"I know it's difficult," Beth said, reaching out her hand to Mom.

"What—What shall we do? What do we do?" Mom looked around desperately, as if an answer might be found printed along the walls.

"We need to admit him—today," Dr. Daly said. "He needs extensive testing, for one thing. And a transfusion."

"Transfusion?" Mom asked. "Why?"

"His platelet count," Dr. Daly said. "He's in a very weakened state. But the platelets will help him recover some energy, maybe even go home eventually."

"He's had transfusions already—he told me, last year," I said.

"According to the records we've had faxed from Dr. Goodson, he's had many," he said. "She was doing her best to keep him going. You can be certain he received the very best care up 'till now."

"My God," Mom said. "How did it get so bad?"

"It's very hard, I know," Beth said, her practiced expression dripping with empathy and understanding. "But he'll be in good hands here. This is the best place for him now."

The next day at the hospital, I sat beside Olaf's bed, staring down at his menu. I glanced up just as Mom returned from the ladies' room. She'd freshened her lipstick, brightening her face to match the hopeful expression she seemed to have conjured in the bathroom mirror. Behind her, a red-cheeked, plump little nurse peeked around the curtain at the stroke of the afternoon shift change. "Charlotte Louise, R.N." was imprinted in bold, upper-case letters on the nametag she'd pinned to the collar of her crisp, white nurses' uniform. Round, gold-rimmed granny glasses clung to the very tip of her button nose.

"I found Charlotte!" Mom said, faking cheerfulness.

"There's my darling!" Charlotte called. "How are we doing today?"

"Doing OK, Charlotte. Thanks."

I stood to give Charlotte more room, fumbling with my oversized bag that had been blocking the narrow walkway. I pressed my back up against the wall, trying to make myself as small as possible in the close quarters.

"Let's get that temp and blood pressure. Open up." Charlotte slipped the thermometer under his tongue and waited for the beep. "I met your Mom. And this is that sister you told me about, right?"

"Yup. Charlotte, Jennifer," Olaf said. "Well, I call her 'Holine'— don't even ask."

"And what's your claim to fame?" Charlotte asked, glancing in my direction.

"Oh, I claim no fame whatsoever," I said. "I'm just this guy's trusty sidekick."

Charlotte held Olaf's wrist, skinny and frail within her chubby grip.

"So what's next?" I asked. "How's he doing?"

"Holding his own," Charlotte said, years of practice enabling her to measure a pulse and still converse. "He's so cute, you wouldn't know he's such a tough cookie. But you're looking a little pale today, Honey. You feeling OK?"

"Just tired," he said. "So tired."

"So, what'd'ya say we try another transfusion?" Charlotte said, taking his hand and nodding along with her motherly advice.

"Ugh," Olaf moaned. "Can't I just stay here?"

"Now, Honey, don't worry," Charlotte said. "I'll fix you all up, nice and comfy. You warm enough?"

Olaf shook his head. He was never warm enough.

"I thought you might be chilly," Charlotte said. "So I brought you a warm blanket—warmed it up just for you on my way in."

Olaf sighed resignedly as Charlotte spread the blanket over him and tucked it in tightly at his sides. I looked at Mom who struggled to control the rising alarm that flashed across her face.

"You need some platelets, my man," Charlotte said, "and I just happen to have some with your name on 'em. Come on, now. Gonna get you downstairs and back up here in no time. Your partner-in-crime here can come along. And Mom, of course."

Charlotte wrapped the blood pressure cuff around Olaf's arm, pumped it tighter, and then, adjusting her stethoscope, listened intently. She shot Mom a look of cautious reassurance, wrapped the stethoscope around her neck in one fluid motion, and stood straight, hands on her wide hips.

"A little low, my darling . . . just a little low," she said, grabbing a clip-boarded chart to make a notation. "Yup, let's get you downstairs. The sooner you get this transfusion, the better you'll feel. I'll get you a wheelchair."

"I'm sure I can walk," Olaf protested. He made a feeble attempt to sit up straight, then collapsed back on his pillows.

"I know you can. But let's save your strength this time around," Charlotte said. "Next time maybe you can walk down. Be right back with that wheelchair." She hustled out, her un-scuffed white shoes squealing across the linoleum.

Olaf shrugged, giving Mom and me a long, sad look, eyes like overcast skies. Mom wasn't literally wringing her hands, but she may as well have been. Her mask of support dissolved in a pool of concern.

"I know it's discouraging, but she's just trying to give you a boost," I said. "We all need a boost sometimes, right? No sense over-exerting yourself. And you'll feel better once it's over."

"I know you're right. I'm just so tired. I don't want to move."

"We'll be with you," I said, taking his hand.

Charlotte returned with the wheelchair, pushed it beside the bed, and helped Olaf to slide his legs over the side. With one arm around his waist and the other guiding his arm, she gently coaxed him into the seat. I stifled a gasp when I caught sight of his frail, thin frame through the gaping hospital gown. It was the frame of an old man, not a 41-year-old, not my brother. With his back to us as we headed to the elevator, Mom pulled a crumpled tissue from her left sleeve and dabbed at the corner of her eyes. She'd seen it too.

Chapter Sixteen
1993-1994

I try to tighten my heart into a knot, a snarl. I try to learn to live dead, just numb . . .

—Tony Kushner, *Angels in America: Part One—Millennium Approaches: A Gay Fantasia on National Themes*

"Holine! *Listen!*" Olaf whispered. "The music!" He tilted his head toward the sound and narrowed his eyes in concentration, straining to hear. Then his mouth curled into his most delighted smile. He nodded knowingly.

"The *music!*" I said, and, dropping my fork, I wriggled out of my seat at the dinner table to spy out the window through the narrow patch of yard between two houses next-door. "The lights just came on!"

"Ma, can we go?" Olaf said, already jumping from his seat and sprinting toward the closet where, on a hook toward the back, our ice skates hung.

"Oh, all right," she said. "Off you go." She fake scowled as we abandoned the roast beef and mashed potatoes that had grown cold on our plates, but her eyes were smiling.

I pulled on my snow pants, still damp from the walk home from school, from a hanger inside the closet door and yanked them up over my pants and sweater, catching the zipper in my haste. "Mittens!" I called. "Where are my mittens?"

"I put them on the register to dry," Mom said. I rushed into the living room and retrieved my and Olaf's mittens, now warm and rigid, hardened in the spots where tiny ice crystals had embedded in the threads. Then I ran toward the back door where Olaf was already lacing his skates in the entryway. I shimmied next to him on the step, slipped my feet in my hand-me-down, double-bladed skates and pulled at the laces.

"Here, lemme do it," he said, and crouching in front of me, pulled the laces tighter, starting at the bottom and cinching them tight as he pulled upward. "Gotta be real tight—you don't want to break an ankle, Holine."

"Kids! Home by eight," Dad said. "School night."

I stood, adjusting to my teetering feet, and wobbled out the door behind Olaf through the backyard path and down the alley to the playground, grabbing at the back of his jacket when I stumbled into a rut in the dark. The cold stung my nostrils as snow fell lightly around us. *Waltz of the Flowers* crackled through the ancient speakers as we approached, the lights around the tennis-court-turned-ice-rink beckoning neighborhood kids from all directions. Kids in puffy nylon coats, some already in skates like us, slipped and slid through the pathways toward the rink. Other kids' skates hung around their necks by laces draped over wooly scarves of red, gold and blue. I slipped my mittened hand through the chain link fence, holding tight at the moment my skates hit the ice, just to get a feel for its slick surface. Then I let go, grabbing the end of Olaf's scarf that he'd unwound from his neck and held out with one hand.

"*Eeeee!*" I shrieked, gliding along behind Olaf as he did the work, thrusting one skate sideways, and then another, with all his strength. He glanced back, grinning wildly, pushing harder and faster.

As we crossed into the far end of the rink, he cried, "Now!" I flung the scarf to the side. My momentum carried me forward directly into the snow bank at the end of the rink, stopping my skates with a thud as I plunged forward into the snow. Like every other kid in the neighborhood, we never bothered to learn how to stop on skates. It was much more fun to soar headlong into the waiting banks of fluffy snow.

"Again! Again!" I shouted, and struggled to right myself. I grabbed for the edge of Olaf's scarf and hauled myself up, eager for the return trip across the ice.

Olaf blinked his eyes open as the TV screen lit up, bathed in white from the snowy mountain backdrop, the harsh light jolting me back to adulthood. I scooched my chair closer to Olaf's hospital bed. He stirred, rising slightly as if lifted on the swell of a wave—like a body surfer, sailing upward toward the crest and straining with all his strength to hang on. From the TV speakers, a tympani boomed a simple marching beat; trumpets burst forth, ringing in the stately Olympic theme.

"Did I miss it? Did she skate yet?"

"No, Honey," I said. "No skating—just skiing, so far."

"Hmmm," he muttered and settled back on his pillow. On TV, Nancy Kerrigan was warming up on the Olympic ice at Lillehammer, her delicate figure floating elegantly into camel spins and spirals, then picking up speed before lurching upward into a triple lutz.

The Winter Olympics figure skating competition, our brother-sister holy ritual, was moments away. Olaf fought to keep his eyes open. And I, having skated on my edges for weeks, fell back in my chair, exhausted from trying, day-after-day, to reawaken him.

"I still can't believe someone would do that—attack her like that," he said, his voice a groggy half-whisper. "All those years, all that hard work . . . "

"I know, I said. "So . . . just . . . *barbaric*."

"So sad. All that practicing, all in vain."

"I wouldn't count her out," I said. "Her short program was flawless."

"Hmmm," he said. "Good, good . . . " His voice faded and he was gone again, the swell subsiding, the wave pulling him under. The pattern had become familiar.

I watched him sleep, studying his face the way I study maps before a trip, attempting to memorize the beauty mark on his upper left cheek, the scar above his lip from the time he'd stumbled into a revolving record on Dad's RCA Victor turntable, the ghost of a one-sided dimple that surfaced when he found something ridiculously funny. I took in the shock of thick, straight hair that fell over his forehead as he slept, and in the half light, he looked fresh and innocent, so much so, I wanted to shake him awake so he would not miss the Olympics—or the rest of his life. Instead, I pulled the remote from the side of his rumpled sheets and pushed the button. The TV went dark. I could not watch without him.

It seemed years earlier, but it had only been two months since Charlotte stopped into Olaf's room, her chubby fingers curled over a clip-boarded chart, granny glasses perched on the end of her nose. A broad smile spread across her rosy face, as she gave us the news. "Dearest," she said, glancing down at the chart, then back at him, "Your platelet count . . . *passable!* And your other numbers—stable."

"What marvelous news!" Mom said, and she beamed at Charlotte.

"Well, if you like that," Charlotte began, "You're gonna love this one: You're going home!"

"Home? Olaf said, his eyes bright. "I . . . *really?*"

"Oh, Olaf," I said. "Just in time for Christmas!"

"Home!" Mom said, the only word she could manage, her voice cracking, her eyes filling with tears.

"Now, don't go crazy," Charlotte warned. "You have to rest, drink at least one Ensure a day, two if you can stomach it." Olaf mimicked a finger down his throat, making clear his opinion of the medicinal excuse for a milkshake. "I know you're not a fan, but Honey—you wanna go home, you follow my orders. Capeesh?'"

"I'll drink pond water if it means I can go home," Olaf said. "Not that this four-star guesthouse you got here is half bad."

"Well, three stars anyway, huh?" Charlotte laughed. "I'll get your paperwork going so we can spring ya', probably tomorrow. Meantime, behave yourself." Charlotte gave Olaf's leg a gentle shake through the covers. Then, just as she headed toward the door, she motioned me to follow as she left the room.

"Jennifer," she gazed intently into my eyes, and whispered, "I know how much you guys wanted him home for Christmas, but keep a close watch. And call the minute he needs anything, or . . . you know, if he seems . . . distant."

"I will," I said. "But, is he really—he's well enough? He's better?"

"He's well enough for a while," she murmured. Then, under her breath, she added, "How long? That's the question, isn't it?"

At Mom and Dad's, Olaf settled into the fold-out couch in the ten-by-ten den, snuggled under a blue-and-white plaid electric blanket. The room, bathed with the muted light of

December, spoke to us of Christmas, the early evening dusk giving way to the twinkling colored lights Dad had lovingly strung around the tree. With Sinatra's *Christmas Waltz* on repeat, Mom sang off-key as she rolled cookie dough into bite-sized treats while the oven released the scent of ginger and cloves and chocolate, bathing us in warmth. It was easy to be lulled into believing all manner of miracles when the spirit was so potent an intoxicant.

Only Olaf's head was visible above the swirl of folds he'd wrapped around his neck to counteract chills that came in waves. He poked a hand out and played a bit of air-piano on the cover of an unopened book in front of him. I sat across from him in the ancient rocker, staring down at the TV tray scattered with winter-term student essays, unable to concentrate.

"I think I told you this, Holine . . . did I?" Olaf asked. "Sorry," he said. "Sometimes my memory isn't so good anymore."

"Told me what?"

"About my piano," he said. "The one I bought secondhand—the Hardman?"

"Yeah, I remember. A couple years ago, right?"

"I couldn't believe I found it. It's old, but they don't make 'em like that anymore. The sound—just *gorgeous*." He shut his eyes, and he was miles away, in Atlanta, as if hearing the piano from a distance. "I miss playing it so much. And I just keep thinking: I wish Sara could have it."

Taken aback at the suggestion, I struggled to respond. Until that moment, Olaf had not mentioned any of the meager possessions he'd left gathering dust in his Atlanta apartment—certainly not his most prized, his beloved piano. So caught up were all of us in the day-to-day—appointments penciled on the calendar, which drug to take at what time—I'd never given a thought about his belongings, all those future orphans that might never find someone to cherish them as he had: his *Missa Solemnis* recording, Teddy's Cubs hat, printed programs from countless performances, the framed photo of his Italian class, the gold chain I'd given him one Christmas. Artifacts of Olaf—each one holding a secret story, a fragment of a jubilant, breathtaking, heart-wrenching *life*.

But the piano. The suggestion that he give it up was an acknowledgement: he understood he would not be returning to Atlanta.

He drifted off, hearing music in his head, counting the beats, playing each part.

"Oh, Holine! That piano—the tone . . . the touch of the keys . . . " He stared forward at the white wall and held his fingers curved above his book, as if straining to feel the keys under his fingers.

"I know you'd love for her to have it," I said. "Maybe we can find a way." I leaned forward and brushed back shiny brown strands of his hair that had fallen across his forehead.

"I guess it's too hard, right now anyway . . . " His voice trailed off, the suggestion more a wistful hope at a time when we were overwhelmed with getting through the day—and hoping to reach the next.

Like tightrope walkers inching across twisted wires, Mom, Dad, Paul, Olaf, and I trod warily through the holidays, intent on pretending that it was just another Christmas even as Olaf spent most of Christmas week cocooned in his blanket, sipping Ensure from a straw. On Christmas Eve, Mom and I made the antipasto—a jumble of romaine and iceberg lettuce, cherry tomatoes, red onion, black and kalamata olives, slivered carrots and black pepper croutons—and piled it high in a huge earthenware bowl, the very Tuscan pottery Olaf had purchased in a countryside shop in the hills above Florence. He had gently folded layers of *La Repubblica* around it and carried it on his lap throughout the ten-hour flight back to JFK. Mom's Christmas present from Olaf. But that was two Christmases ago.

Mom and I fried shrimp and haddock and sole, and finally Dad's smelt, which he had netted, cleaned, and frozen in Tupperware as he did every spring. At dinner, Olaf pushed the delicacies around on his plate—this meal he had once so enjoyed—as if he were a child again, trying to hide the fact that he hadn't eaten a bite.

On Christmas afternoon, Olaf rallied, even summoning the energy to play *War* with Sara. He layered a sweatshirt over his pajama top, then dealt the all the cards. When he'd finished, he and Sara began frantically flipping them.

"War!" Olaf squealed as he overturned a jack-of-hearts next to Sara's jack-of-clubs. Sara straightened her stack, readying it for the showdown. "Ya-ha-ha!" Olaf chuckled his most sinister laugh, and counted down as they overturned each card. "One, two, three, four, five, flip!" His face dropped in fake disappointment as he revealed his deuce, and Sara flashed her winning ten-of-diamonds, then greedily raked in her winning cards.

She flipped again, a queen of clubs, as Olaf, with a dramatic flourish, produced a king of hearts. "Ha—so you finally won one, Uncle!" Sara said.

For a moment, Olaf stared blankly at the cards. He picked up the king of hearts, examining it—one side, then the other. He handed it to Sara.

"Think I . . . um . . . " he began, looking from the card deeply into her face. "Sara Beth?" he asked, then touched her gently on the cheek as if making sure she was real. "Maybe I . . . I think I might need a nap."

"Sore loser! Sore loser!" she cried, victorious.

Olaf scooched into the couch, and, pulling his blanket tight around him, he turned onto his right side, facing away from us.

The kids and I spent every day of Christmas vacation with Olaf at Mom and Dad's until it was dark and bitter cold when I finally dragged them home for bed. The weeks ran together, a blur of cooking and TV and card-playing. When Olaf napped, I scrambled to meet my class and grade papers or dashed home to do a load of laundry and let the dog out. I slept hard, my dreams a tangle of memories and worries that shook me awake. Then I rose and began a frantic rush toward Mom and Dad's, half-crazy until I could see Olaf for myself. For a few weeks, every day was the same. Until it wasn't.

I sat up in bed, pushed the hair out of my eyes. For a moment, I didn't realize what had awakened me.

Then a second shrill *rrrring.*

I reached over Paul for the phone.

"Hello?" I whispered.

"Jen . . . "

The voice, a raspy whisper, didn't sound like anyone I knew.

The person on the other end cleared his throat.

"Jen. It's Dad," he said. "I'm sorry . . . " Then, nothing, followed by a muffled *whoosh,* as if he had slid his hand over the receiver.

"Dad? What, what's happening?"

"I . . . uh . . . we need you." Again, nothing.

I heard him struggle to swallow a sob.

Then he said, "It's your brother. I've called an ambulance. Please, can you come? Please? Your mother, she just — she can't do it."

"I'll be right there," I said. I threw on the jeans I'd slung over my dresser the night before, and pulled a sweatshirt from a hanger.

Paul sat up in bed. "What's happening?"

"It's Olaf," I sighed. "Dad called an ambulance. I have to go."

"But what . . . " Paul began.

"I don't know what happened. Only—he sounded desperate."

"I'll come with you," Paul said and began to rise

"No—you need to stay," I said. "The kids are still sleeping."

"I don't like you going alone." He hesitated, then rose from the bed, following me to the back door. "Make sure you call me."

"I'll keep you posted," I said, and grabbed my purse, slid on my coat and ran out the door.

When I arrived at Mom and Dad's, Olaf was sitting at the dining room table. He looked right through me, staring straight ahead. And said nothing. Dad, his face an open wound, fought back tears as he paced between the kitchen window and the dining room, checking for the ambulance, then checking on Olaf, then back to the window.

I sprinted into the dining room and pulled a chair close to Olaf's.

"You OK, Honey?" I asked. When he didn't answer, I reached for his hand, but he was unresponsive, his hand lifeless in mine. He still said nothing, just stared straight ahead, as though he had moved on somewhere. Dad rushed back into the room when he heard a siren in the distance.

"They're here," he said. He turned to Olaf. "You ready?"

Olaf did not look at him, just stared ahead. Dad picked up the small zippered bag he had packed for Olaf and went to the door, just as two ambulance attendants burst through it.

"The patient?" said the first.

"This way," Dad said, and led them to the dining room. I let go of Olaf's hand and moved aside. The first attendant, Jim, knelt in my place.

"Hey there, buddy," he said gently as he reached for Olaf's hand. "We're gonna help you now. I'm just gonna take your pulse here, OK? Just feeling your wrist here a moment. There you go." Jim took Olaf's wrist and waited. "Let me just get your blood pressure. Here you go, now. Just gonna feel a little squeeze." He fitted the blood pressure cuff around Olaf's arm and pumped it tight, then listened intently through his stethoscope. "On the low side," he said. "Feeling poorly, huh? You passed out?"

Olaf looked blankly at Jim and didn't answer. So Dad said, "He had a rough night. He was confused; we heard noises upstairs, and in the den—he had a lighter—and I'm not sure what he thought he was lighting. Then he just collapsed. We didn't know what to do."

"It's OK now," Jim said, sparing Dad the need to fill in any more details.

"His pills," Dad said. "I have all his pills, and his schedule, this schedule I made for him." His voice broke as he passed the chart to Jim, seeming not ready to relinquish it.

Jim tucked the sheet in his pocket, then turned to Olaf. "These little lapses happen sometimes, right?" he asked gently, looking into Olaf's eyes. "We got cha' now, buddy. Just gonna give you a little ride back to Upstate, OK?"

Still, Olaf did not speak. He stared into the distance, as if seeing something we could not.

"I'm his sister," I said. "Can I ride along?" Not thinking clearly, I'd forgotten I was going to the hospital alone.

"Better to follow," Jim said. "You know . . . in case he's admitted."

Jim's expression made clear: Olaf would be admitted.

The second attendant rolled in a stretcher and unfolded it in one easy motion. Then he and Jim tenderly coaxed Olaf from his seat at the table and helped him onto the stretcher, tucked a blanket around him and belted him in.

"Meet us at the ER," Jim said, stopping when he saw my alarmed expression. His warm blue eyes looked straight into mine. "I know," he said. "I promise: we'll take good care of him."

I stood in the doorway, watching as the attendants wheeled Olaf to the back of the ambulance and hoisted the stretcher upward and in. Then the lights began to flash. The ambulance turned the corner, and they were gone.

"Dad," I said, "what exactly happened? And where's Mom?"

"She was up all night," he said. "Your brother was . . . he's confused. She, she tried talking to him. She pleaded with him, but it was like he couldn't hear or even *see* us. And he was agitated, moving things around, like he was looking for something. And then, there was this lighter."

"What do you mean, lighter?" I said. "He had a lighter?" Dad looked down at the floor, as if trying to find an answer there. "Dad. They're going to ask me. At the hospital. They'll need to know."

"There was some . . . he was disturbed," Dad said. "He tried to light something, burned the edge of the toilet seat somehow . . . " Dad gazed at his feet. A tear slid down his cheek. He hastily wiped it away with the back of his sleeve.

I walked into the den where Olaf had been sleeping on the fold-out for the last several weeks. Items were overturned and out-of-place; the couch was slightly askew. I poked my head into Mom's bedroom, but she lay silent and still, her eyes forced closed. I ran into the bathroom and looked around. On the edge of the toilet seat was an oblong scorch, a gray blemish marring the polished white surface.

Never straying from the passing lane, I drove through a blur of lights, flashing signs, thruway toll booths, and intermittent snow, praying the chant-like prayers taught to me in childhood—*Hail Mary, full of grace, Hail Mary, full of grace.* The words came to me like a snippet of a song that repeats in a loop, the only break in my mantra an occasional expletive when a timid driver pulled into my lane to avoid a plow or 18-wheeler. As I glanced at the thruway ticket and dug for exact change with my right hand—glancing down and up again, down and up again—I pictured Olaf arriving at the hospital without me, confused, wondering why he was alone. Pressing the accelerator harder, my prayers became more frantic, matching my increasing speed. *Hail Mary, hail Mary, hail Mary . . .* On the dash was the magnetized miniature St. Christopher that Olaf had given me when I bought my first car.

I parked in a massive lot, then trudged through snowy ruts and to the door of the Emergency Room. Frost formed a lacy pattern around the edge of sliding doors that opened as I approached, and a gust of warm Pine Sol-tinged air was sucked outside, hitting me full in the face. Inside, I proceeded down a dim corridor, its floor glistening with wax, my boots squeaking their wet soles over the surface. At the intake desk, a dour-faced nurse peeked through a ten-inch rectangular hole in her plexiglass cubicle.

"And you are?" she demanded. I looked down at her lapel where her Health Science Center badge declared her to be R. Schmidt, RN.

"Hi, I'm here for my brother, um . . . he just got here. Amcare from Rome?" "Yeah—they're getting him settled now." She reached for a clipboard on her counter, then slid it through the opening. "Here—fill out this paperwork for him. They say he can't manage it."

"I'm . . . a," I began. "I have his health insurance card here." I dug in my purse for Olaf's cards and paperwork, which I'd kept for him since his first admission.

"Already on file," she barked. "Just fill out the forms," and she turned to answer the ringing phone.

I waded through pages of questions—family medical history, insurance queries, medications lists, emergency contacts. When I'd completed all I could, I returned the clipboard to Nurse Schmidt, who droned into the phone pressed against her ear but made no gesture of acknowledgement toward me. I had no choice but to sit back down and wait for a chance to ask where they'd taken Olaf.

Finally, Nurse Schmidt slammed down the phone and sighed heavily. I rushed to the desk.

"Yes?" she snapped.

"My brother," I said. "I'd like to see him."

"Can't just yet," she said. "They're still getting him settled."

"So how long 'till . . . " I began.

"Here," she said and handed me a sticky note and a pen. "Give me your name, and I'll call you when he's set." I wrote my name and handed it back.

I turned back to the row of plastic chairs and picked up a battered *Time* magazine from the pile on a rack that separated them, turning the pages, my eyes glossing over the words. Several new patients arrived; spouses and mothers and fathers and partners rushed through paperwork, and were called, one after another, to the bedside of a loved one, as the minutes—and then hours—ticked by. By this time, my head pounded from lack of caffeine, food and sleep. Finally, I approached Nurse Schmidt again.

"Please," I said. "I've waited hours. Can't I see my brother now?"

"You are?"

"Yes, Jennifer—remember me?" I said. "You said you'd let me know when I could see my brother?"

"Oh, yeah," she said. "They're still doing some tests."

"What? What tests?"

"The doctor will fill you in when he makes rounds," she said. "Now, please. I will call you," she said sternly, then turned back to the stack of papers on the desk.

Reluctantly, I wheeled around to the row of seats, but couldn't will myself back down. I wandered to a waiting room at the end of the hallway where half-empty vending machines lined one wall. I found a pay phone and called to check on the kids, but no one answered. With no other options, I ambled back to my seat in front of the nurses' station, and, giving in, drifted off to sleep.

At the sound of my name, I jumped, realizing I'd dozed off. With one hand, I rubbed my neck, stiff from the hard plastic chair.

"You can come in now," Nurse Schmidt announced and motioned toward a door at the far end of the waiting room. Another nurse appeared in the doorway and held the door open for me. I followed her down a corridor where she left me in an oversized hospital room, one usually reserved for two or three patients. In the center, a tiny Olaf lay on a rolling bed. He was covered in white—sheets, blanket, even the skin over his face. As I walked to the head of the bed, I saw it: a single jaundiced tear streamed down the side of his face.

"Holine," he cried. "Where did you go?"

"They wouldn't let me in, Honey," I said. "But I've been right here the whole time."

"Oh, Holine," he said, then whispered, "They were mean to me." Just then, a nurse breezed in. Olaf was suddenly quiet.

Maybe it was the effect of the medicinal fumes that permeated the air or the reek of heavy disinfectants. But suddenly, the metallic taste of blood raged on my tongue. Seething, my eyes wide with fury, I began to shout, "Excuse me, are you the one supposedly caring for my brother?" but Olaf shot me a look of warning and shook his head, communicating without words the way we always had: *Careful . . . If we complain, I could pay later.*

The nurse looked up at me blandly. "You family?" she asked.

"Yes," I said. "I'm his sister. And I've been waiting hours to see him. Please, what is going on?"

"Well, he's being admitted," she said with a sigh. "Meet us up in room 408. The doc will be along."

"Now?"

"Yes, now," she said and turned toward the door. "Come on, big fella," she said to a burly orderly who appeared in the doorway. "Let's get this guy upstairs." On their way out, I heard her mutter in disgust, "Yup, we got another one. Keep your mask and gloves handy."

I felt my face redden with rising anger and pressed my lips together to stifle my rage at the heartless nurse, at the sluggish hospital, at the Earth, at the sky. I took a step forward and watched as Olaf was wheeled away.

Through the maze of hallways and connective tunnels, I found room 408. I peeked through the doorway to find a cluster of medically-clad personnel surrounding Olaf, one pumping his bed upright, another handing him a tiny paper cup and instructing him to swallow a capsule, a third poking his right hand, connecting him through a plastic tube to an IV tower. Seeing me waiting in the hallway, a nurse approached, then asked me to wait in a tiny room containing only a two-seat couch, a straight chair, and a TV. When she finally reappeared and ushered me to Olaf's room, he was already asleep.

"He's out, I'm afraid," she said. "He's been through it all today . . . and given the sedative, no way he wakes up. I suggest you go home and get some rest." She looked into my anxious eyes and added, "It's OK. He'll be here tomorrow."

The next day, I left work at lunchtime and picked up Mom to drive her to the hospital. It became our pattern for the next month or so: I worked for a half day, long enough for me to see three or four students and teach my class, then took a half day of sick leave, Mom and I settling in at the hospital until we were chased out as visiting hours ended.

It was an unspoken understanding among me, Mom and Dad that Dad would never come; he never could stand it when one of us was sick. Knowing he would fall apart if he visited the hospital, Mom and I did our best to conjure excuses that we knew were lies—his arthritis was acting up; he had a bad cold. It was better for us all that he stayed away. The sight of him breaking down would have been too much.

When Mom and I arrived at the hospital, we were surprised to find Olaf alert and sitting up in bed. The color had returned to his cheeks.

"Olaf!" I said. "You look so much better today!" Mom rushed to his bedside and kissed him warmly on the cheek.

"Honey," she said. "How're you doing?"

"Better, Ma," he said. "Just so, so tired. Yesterday was hell. I can't believe I'm back here already."

"Well, the good news is, you're back on four," I said.

"Yes, see that?" Mom said. "We'll get Charlotte again."

"Oh, she's already been here," he said. "My personal escort for a transfusion—thus the girlish glow." He pointed to his newly rosy cheeks.

"Well, you look a hundred percent better," Mom said. "And so alert!"

"Yeah, Ma," Olaf looked down at his hands. "Sorry about that. I don't remember much about that night."

"It's all behind us now," she said, patting his hand gently.

"I didn't do, you know," he began, "Anything scary?"

"No, no," she said. "We were just worried, that's all."

A cart rattled its way down the hall and into his room.

"Lunchtime, dah-ling!" the orderly announced, set the food on Olaf's tray table and raised it in one fluid motion, sliding it in front of Olaf. "Need help?"

"Nah," Olaf said. "My sister here will help me out." Then to me he said, "This is Mark—he's one of the good ones."

"Now, don't let me come back here and find food left on that plate!" Mark said. "You need *nour-ish-ment*. Get me?" Mark nodded emphatically, flashed a bright smile, then sprinted back to his cart, squeaking its rusty wheels further down the hallway.

"Well, I missed my second cup, so I'm gonna go find a cup of coffee," Mom said. "You want anything, Jen?"

"No, I'm fine."

"Be right back," Mom said. I knew the coffee was an excuse; Mom had gone off in search of a nurse or a doctor in a futile attempt to shed some light on what had caused Olaf's confusion. She wanted reassurance; she wanted answers. She wanted a miracle.

I took the cover off Olaf's meal, and he reached weakly for a limp half of grilled cheese. "Some lunch," he said. Then, "Hey, ya wanna fill out my menu for tomorrow for me?"

"Sure," I said. "But I hope you know, I'm checking every box." While I pondered the choices—mac and cheese or meatloaf, pudding or yogurt—Olaf chewed half-heartedly, then dropped the half-eaten sandwich back on the tray.

"So, Holine," he said, pausing to find the right words. "I'm glad Mom's off tracking down coffee or whatever. I wanted a chance to—you know—for just us, to talk."

"Good," I said. "Is there something I can do? Something you need?"

"No," he said. "It's not that. It's just, I worry about you."

"About me? Why? I'm fine."

"I don't mean now," he said. "I'm worried about what will happen to you. When I'm gone."

Stunned by words that acknowledged, out loud, that he was dying, I looked into his eyes. That word—*gone*—as if he would just vanish one day. His eyes filled with tears, not for himself but for me.

"I'll be OK," I lied. "I have the kids, my family. Work. I'll be OK, really."

He looked at me as if he'd been stung. The rush of new tears in my eyes, I searched in vain for the right thing to say. But all I could think of was the truth. That I dreaded each morning when that sweet, oblivious moment between sleeping and waking dissolved into reality, and I realized once again that my brother was dying. That every day, I pasted myself back together and forced myself forward. That nothing would ever be OK again.

Instead, I reached out my hand to hold his and said nothing.

Chapter Seventeen
1994

There is no vaccine in sight . . . The epidemic continues to spread relentlessly across the globe. It has killed 210,000 people in the United States alone and eviscerated entire subcultures, including the arts community, which gives depth and resonance to the rest of the population. It is a new disease that has turned the world old overnight.

—Natalie Angier, Anthony S. Fauci: Consummate Politician on the AIDS Front, *The New York Times*

Sue unwound the damp towel, releasing dripping strands of my newly-dyed hair that fell randomly around my shoulders. As she brushed it vigorously away from my face, she looked at me skeptically, then pressed her lips together to suppress the comment that would wait there, unspoken till I returned for my next visit. Sue was much more than my hairstylist; she had become my close friend and confidant, someone who knew me at least as well as I knew myself. She gently curved my hair around a round brush, the warmth of the blow dryer revealing the transformation—my formerly blonde hair returned to its natural brown. I surveyed the straight, chestnut locks in the salon mirror, ran my fingers through the newly-trimmed ends, blunt and even, like the edge of a paint brush grazing my fingertips. I felt both young and old at once.

I left the salon and drove the few blocks to Mom's where she was waiting as always, already bundled in her coat and boots, her nose pressed against the window for who knows how long. As she walked toward the car, gingerly avoiding the random patches of ice scattered across the plowed sidewalk, I adjusted the rearview mirror. For a moment, I did a doubletake as I glimpsed an unfamiliar darkened profile that caught the corner of my eye. I'd already forgotten that my hair was brown, the color of my hair as a child. I looked like I did in those 1970's Polaroids stacked in a box in Mom's attic—younger again—me and Olaf, arm-in-arm. But all I'd managed to change was my hair color. It wasn't 1970; it was 1994. And my brother was still dying.

At the hospital Olaf dozed in a stark white room, airless and stale, the medicinal smell of antiseptic mixing with ammonia, not quite masking the miasma of illness. Mom kissed him gently on the forehead, then she and I took our positions beside him—I, closer to the foot of the bed. His fever had subsided some. His body beneath the blankets was diminished, reminding me of one of his childhood pranks: toys bunched under the covers to mimic a human form after Olaf had fled through the open window to a private spot on the roof. I'd found him there, reclining on a pillow and shining a flashlight on his copy of *Huckleberry Finn*. How I wished the small, bundled form before me was a ruse, the real Olaf elsewhere.

Mom sat silently staring at him, assuming her usual expression: bewildered despair. Every so often, she turned to me with eyes that seemed to plead, *Do something*, only to be met by my blank, hopeless face. In the background *Dog Day Afternoon* played on a black-and-white TV that hung from metal brackets facing Olaf's bed.

Olaf stirred and mouthed weakly, "Oh…you're here." Then, sighing deeply, he turned to me and said, "Is it yet another day?" I nodded in response and squeezed his hand. I watched his face contort as he struggled to summon the last of his determination. He gathered himself as if bundling together his limbs, like a cord cinched around kindling. He bent forward, straining for strength, and slid one leg laboriously across the bed, as if strapped to it was a hundred-pound weight. Then he did the same with the other, dropped his feet to the floor and stood.

"Now, now, my friend," Charlotte, who had some kind of Olaf radar, said, swooping in, seemingly out of nowhere. "You know you're supposed to use the call button if you want to get up." She was beside him in seconds, one arm around his waist, the other reaching for the walker. "Boy's room, Honey?" she asked. Olaf nodded weakly and inched his way to the bathroom.

While they were gone, I scouted a vending machine and bought a Coke, then stopped off at the ladies' room. As I was returning to Olaf's hospital room, I stopped short, then stepped back, out of sight. Through the doorway I noticed Mom had moved from her usual spot and was hovering over Olaf, her arms wrapped around him; her face, tender, tormented. "It's OK, Honey," she said. "Mommy's here." Olaf's eyes fluttered, then opened, and he looked into her face, brightening suddenly.

"Mama," he mumbled, and gave a half smile. "My grandfather," he said, shaking his head as if the two of them were in on some private joke.

"No," she said, tilting her head to the side, worried about his mistake, confused herself. "Mama."

"Yes, but…" Olaf laughed. "Grandpa . . . he keeps calling to me: 'Andiamo! Andiamo!'" Then, awakening further, Olaf looked at Mom, startled, as though he'd given away a secret meant only for him.

"No, Honey," she said. "Just me. Pa died seven years ago, remember? *I'm* here." She held him, rocking him gently as if he were a baby again, and he slid back into sleep. Finally, Mom returned to her chair. She sat with her face in her hands. I tiptoed back to my seat.

Olaf drifted in and out of sleep and seemed unaware of our presence for the rest of the day. Finally, a disembodied voice announced authoritatively through a muffled speaker, "It's eight p.m. Visiting hours are now over." Mom peeked out the hospital door to see if we could get away with staying a little longer, but a nurse making her rounds spotted her and motioned toward the clock. We bundled into our layers of scarves, gloves and puffy coats, and took turns kissing Olaf's damp cheek. Mom lingered, taking a last long look.

We rode in silence. I concentrated on my driving, maneuvering east on the slippery highway narrowed by snow that had been falling for days. The car's wipers swished and whined; snow glistened on the blacktop surface; a battalion of plows blocked the passing lane. I slowed down, not trusting the Dodge's front-wheel drive, despite wanting desperately to be home, knowing there would be laundry and housework before I could finally ease myself into my warm bed.

"You have to wonder," I said, "how long a person can possibly go on like this." Startled by my own words, I realized that I'd actually said this out loud, this thought that had been cycling in my head for days. She shot me a look. She said nothing, but her accusing eyes spoke her question.

"I mean . . . so much suffering . . . " I trailed off, lost in the anguish of knowing Olaf's death was inevitable yet wanting him with us as long as he could hold on, hoping his suffering would end while dreading its end. I was exhausted by this silent death watch. Every day Olaf becoming smaller, leaving us one cell at a time, when what I wanted most was *not* to sit quietly. What I wanted was to rant and scream and rage. And then to sleep—to sink into oblivion, to make it stop.

"You know," I said, surprising us both by the sound of my voice, "I have to believe that there is someone or something watching over us. I feel it—not a guardian angel or anything exactly—but . . . a presence." I realized I was just babbling, but the silence was so oppressive, I couldn't stop myself. Maybe I said it to console her, a futile attempt to penetrate the darkness that had expanded the distance between us.

"I don't," she snapped back. "I'm beginning to believe that *no one* is watching over us. How can I ever believe a thing like that now?" She did not stifle a sob, did not reach for the tissue that she always had handy. Instead, she set her face in anger, outraged that she, of all people, could lose her own son. She stared forward out the windshield where the steady spray of snowflakes disintegrated into droplets of water and clung to the glass for a split second, only to be wiped away.

I stopped talking.

I dropped Mom off, watched her walk inside and shut the back door behind her. When I finally got home, I kicked off my boots and heaved my bookbag on the counter. Dishes were piled in the sink. Down the hall, Sara and Paul Joe were already asleep in their beds; I'd missed kissing them good-night again. Paul was on couch, the newspaper propped in front of him. I sank into the chair across from him.

"How's he doing?" he asked.

"He was hardly awake all day."

"I'm sorry, Jen," he said sadly. He put the paper down and turned toward me, reaching his hand toward mine. I moved closer to him and held his hand a moment.

"I just don't know how long he can go on like this. Or, how long I can."

"You can't think like that," he said. "Just—you know—one day at a time."

"I'm just . . . I'm so tired of watching him slip away. It's like, every day, there's a little less of him."

"I know, Jen, " he said. "Look. The kids are settled for the night. The house, grading your papers—everything can wait."

"I know, but if I get even more behind . . . "

"You're killing yourself. You don't want to get sick, do you?"

"Me? I can't afford to get sick."

"So, why don't you try to get some sleep? Take care of yourself, just for one night."

"Maybe you're right." I dragged myself off the couch toward the bedroom.

I found my nightgown in the closet, then set my jewelry on the nightstand, beside the phone. I sat on the bed and stared down at the phone, considering; then, in a spasm of self-pity, I flipped off the ringer. I peeled back the covers and got into bed, pulling the blanket high over my head. I was asleep in moments.

A voice, robotic and familiar, came out of the distance. " . . . a collect call . . . do you accept . . . " I turned over in my half-sleep, vaguely aware. *Someone there?* But the voice was gone, followed by a sustained beep. Then, nothing. I pulled the pillow over my face and descended into a deep sleep.

Buzz . . . Buzz . . . Buzz!

I turned and hit the snooze button, pulling the covers up to my neck. Only my face was exposed to the morning chill. Wind whipped against the bedroom window and seeped through the cracks. I snuggled deeply under the warm comforter, and dozed.

Buzz . . . buzz.

I hit snooze again, but before I could pull the covers over my head, Paul appeared in the doorway, a mug of coffee in his hand.

"Jen," he said softly. "It's late. You gotta get up."

Defiant, I shut my eyes.

"C'mon, Jen," he said. "Your mother already called."

I slowly pulled myself up and propped the pillows behind me.

"I'm . . . ugh . . . how'm I gonna do this?"

"Here," he said. "Drink this. Oh, and there's a message on the answering machine that makes no sense. Someone called collect or something? I don't know, it was cut off . . . "

"What?" I screamed. "Collect? No one calls me collect except . . . "

I jumped out of bed, ran into the kitchen, and hit rewind on the answering machine. Out of the speaker, a portion of a cut-off message crackled, "a collect call from SUNY Health Science. Do you accept . . . "

"Oh my God!" I yelled. "It was the hospital. Or Olaf. It was Olaf himself. And I missed it! It's all my fault!"

"What do you mean, your fault?" Paul asked. "Jen, you're not making sense."

"*I* did it," I said. "Myself. I was so tired, I turned off the ringer in the bedroom. I just couldn't take any more. And now, what if he needed me? Or worse? What if it's worse?" I cried. I ran into the bedroom, pulling my clothes from the closet and sobbing.

"Calm down," he said, but I rushed past him into the bathroom, a pile of clothes in my hands.

When I was dressed, I called the nurse's station. "No," the on-call nurse said. "No one called you from the medical staff," and "Yes, your brother is resting comfortably at the moment."

But my relief at this news was short-lived; it meant that Olaf himself had called. And I hadn't been there for him.

My frenzied breaths didn't fully subside till I found Olaf dozing in the dusky hospital room, the curtains pulled tight, denying even the dim light of the cloudy, late winter sky. I could barely see him until my eyes adjusted to the dark room. As Mom and I got closer, he blinked awake, jostled by our winter boots clunking against the tiles. Mom rushed to his side and kissed him sweetly.

"Good Sunday morning," she said, rubbing his arm affectionately.

"Is it?" he said. "Morning?" Olaf asked, his eyes bleary.

"March 13," she said. "Almost spring already. But it feels like . . . Oooh, still cold, more like February."

"I, uh . . . " he began. He tried without success to sit up in bed, then slumped back down. "Holine," he began again. "Holine, I tried to call you. Didn't I? A while ago, it was, I think. Or was it yesterday? I'm not sure." He gazed down at his blanket and pulled at the threads, as though the invisible bugs were back, crawling randomly, here and there, all over its surface. Then, he stopped short and looked into my eyes. A wave of understanding passed across his face. That look: it would be tattooed forever on my heart. In a momentary flash, he knew he had made that call. He consciously readjusted his expression, arranging his face to reject the truth — that he'd needed me and I hadn't been there. With one look, he covered for me, signaling his forgiveness. "Oh, never mind," he said sweetly, a pale smile crossing his lips. "I wanted you here, but you're here now, my Holine."

I thought that his forgiveness might crush me.

"Let's get some light in this room," Mom said, vaguely aware that something had transpired. As she pulled the cord alongside the curtains, the drapery-hooks scraped across the rod to expose a view of the parking lot. I looked outside to the scene below through the snowflakes that melted into droplets on the pane, blurring the outlines of arriving visitors, their winter grays and blacks and navys muddled, like a dismal, rain-splattered impressionist painting.

Despite the muted daylight, Olaf sunk more deeply into his pillow and stopped talking entirely, descending into a morphine-laden repose. When I squeezed his hand gently, he ever-so-faintly squeezed back. But he did not speak again that day. Nor ever again.

Without having to explain why, when I'd left her the previous evening, Mom had said, "I think we'd better leave earlier tomorrow. Can you call into work?" So, after the kids left, I went out to start the car and began hurriedly scraping the ice from the Shadow's windshield, cursing myself silently for not starting earlier, sure I'd be keeping Mom waiting.

Instead of her usual anxious face pressed against the window, when I got to the house I found the door still locked, the kitchen window dark. I used my key and let myself in.

"Ma?" I called from the entryway, shaking the snow off my boots. "Ma—you ready?" When she didn't answer, I kicked off my boots and went inside the quiet house, searching for signs of life. I found them in the den: Mom leaning over Dad, who was bent forward on the edge of his chair, his head bowed, his face in his hands.

"Honey," she whispered to him. "It's OK. If you can't do it . . . it's OK." Dad lifted his head and looked desperately into her eyes, then opened his mouth to answer. All he could manage was a stifled sob. He shook his head sadly, burying his face in his hands once again.

"Maybe it's better," Mom said gently. "You'll think of him as he was." She kissed him softly on the top of his head and turned to leave. Looking up one last time, Dad spied me in the doorway. I raised my hand in a quiet wave, a signal of understanding.

All the way to the hospital, between the top-40 hits, the radio's local news played on a loop—school closings in Oswego County, milder temperatures in Central New York, Route 81 backed up from the 690 interchange into downtown—while Mom and I barely spoke. We had run out of things to say, unable to sustain the lies we'd told each other, no longer taking turns spinning narratives that would buoy the other: hopes about transitory platelet counts, excuses about Dad's continued absence from the hospital, possible new medications, guardian angels. None of them worked for us any longer.

We found Beth, the social worker we'd met on our first day at the hospital, sitting with Olaf when we arrived. She was perched in Mom's usual seat, holding Olaf's hand and speaking softly to him, although he seemed unaware of her. She picked up a tiny pink sponge, and, holding it by its tooth-picked end, dipped it in the pitcher of water and gently pressed it against his lips. At the sound of our footsteps, she turned and motioned for Mom to take her place. Still in her winter coat and gloves, Mom sat erect and held the metal base of the chair with both hands, bracing herself.

Olaf, his breathing labored and erratic, was propped up in bed, his hospital gown slightly askew, falling off one shoulder. He appeared paper-thin and lifeless, like the paper dolls of my childhood when a torn tab sent their little dresses tilting to one side.

"It's good that you're here," Beth said. "It's not going to be long now."

Mom gasped, dropped her head.

"W-why . . . " I began. "He's almost sitting up—can that be comfortable?"

"It's his breathing," she said. "The position makes it less difficult for him."

I pulled a chair next to his bed and took his hand, clammy and limp. I squeezed, but, unlike the day before, he did not squeeze back.

"I'll leave you with him," Beth said. "I'm just down the hall if you need me."

Beth was no sooner out the door than Charlotte rushed in.

"Charlotte!" I said. "This isn't your usual shift."

"No, Honey," she said. "Traded. Had to be with my main man today."

"Right," I said, as tears streamed down my face. Mom shot us a look of desperation, as if the insinuation itself was a betrayal. Feeling her despair, Charlotte got down to business, checking Olaf's IV, his fluid levels, his blood pressure. She made the necessary notations on his chart, kissed him lightly on the forehead and walked away, hiding her face from us. Then she was gone, the only sounds were the hum and beep of Olaf's IV and his uneven, raspy breathing.

I looked down at Olaf's hand in mine and thought of the many times he had taken my hand to guide or protect me—hundreds of times he'd walked me across the street to the playground, to the library, to school, to the ice cream stand. This very hand had guided me through crowds of bigger kids to see movies, never caring that he was the only kid at the cinema with his little sister in tow. This hand that glided elegantly across the keys of his piano, then stalled, frozen and stretched, octave-wide, waiting for me to turn the page of his sheet music. This hand that I awoke to, holding mine, after the accident; that led, as he taught me to jitterbug, and that tugged me into the subway, just before the doors slammed shut. I stared down at it, noticing its delicacy, even now: not much bigger than mine.

Slender fingers interlaced with mine.

Chapter Eighteen
2019

You visit me at all hours/while riding on a bus/while shopping for food/while sitting in a theatre/and the whoosh of the ascending/curtain is like your whisper.

—Tom Giordano, *Unending Dialogue: Voices from an AIDS Poetry Workshop*

Sara and her husband Ryan arrived at the house with my grandchildren, Ani and Gordy, for a family dinner. They had just kicked off their shoes and raincoats when Ani ran ahead into the kitchen where she knew she'd find me. I scooped her up, her tiny arms squeezed tightly around my neck as Sara, her eyes sparkling, followed into the kitchen. One-year-old Gordy peeked from behind his father, who held him aloft, piggy-back.

"You have to hear this, Mom," Sara said as she pulled her I-phone from her purse.

"What ya got?" I said. "Some new music or something?"

"Not just anybody's music," she said proudly. "Ryan wrote me a song."

"A song! How sweet is that?"

I swung the dishtowel over my shoulder and looked down at her phone, already queued to the song. Sara hit "play."

The simple song, so uniquely Ryan, resonated with honest, unspoiled love, his words expressing his unconditional devotion for Sara, the depth of feeling that any parent would only hope for her child.

Here it is, everyone standing in line
They say love should be patient and kind
And we've arrived, here as our travels combine
Chance and direction and time
It's a sign, you can't read if you open your eyes
Just move forward with arms open wide

Oh and I'm gonna love you til the wheels come off
Til the wheels come off

So it goes, we danced under firefly light
And the sky is on fire tonight
And I'll try, to find the things we need to get by
Babe we got nothing but time

Oh and I'm gonna love you til the wheels come off
Til the wheels come off

We're all blessed and restless and borrowed and bought and we're sold
We're all unfinished business, reliable witness to love

Oh, and I'm gonna love you til the wheels come off
Til the wheels come off

Just as the song was about to end, Sara said, "Hear that piano? It's Uncle's! Uncle's piano!" Her face bursting with joy, she swayed in time, holding Ani's two hands in hers, then swirling her in a circle. Ani's laughter lilted over the evocative chords, chords emanating from the very same piano keys that had delighted under Olaf's touch, that had been delivered through his last wish and had found their way home to us. Now tucked in the corner of Sara's living room, the piano had been brought back to life, simultaneously restoring to us some of the life we had lost.

And Ryan had written the song proclaiming love that is limitless—the love of a husband for a wife, an uncle for a niece, a brother for a sister.

Epilogue
2020-2024

The one thing we know about epidemics is that at some point, they will end. The one thing we don't know is who we will be then.

—Andrew Sullivan, *New York Magazine*

I lay shivering beneath a weighted blanket, my fever spiking to 101.9. My head throbbed; twinges of pain shot like electrical currents up the back of my neck into my skull. Unable to read, the TV volume on low, I stared blankly at the newscast. Gov. Cuomo had just outlawed large gatherings. Broadway was shutting down. March Madness—cancelled; the NBA—suspended. My cell phone buzzed an alert: our public schools were closing. And now I had become sick.

Across the country, cases of COVID were rising. The sudden illness, rapid decline, and death of formerly healthy persons left doctors and nurses unprepared, overwhelmed . . . and exposed. And all I could think was: *Not again.* For me and countless others who lost loved ones to HIV-AIDS, COVID was not the first lethal viral pandemic of my lifetime, but the second.

From the very first reports in 1981 that a mysterious and deadly illness was afflicting otherwise healthy young gay men, I was consumed with dread. Still, it seemed inconceivable that modern medicine would not solve the mystery of HIV-AIDS. Surely, I thought, scientists would make a discovery, and, in short order, save the dying. However, for the next twelve years, I vacillated between anguish and hope, waiting in vain for a cure—or at the very least, an effective treatment. In 2020, as COVID surged across the world, all my anxieties flooded back. And I had learned not to expect miracles.

Feverish, achy and congested, I dozed on the couch. I awoke to a Trump news briefing on TV. When a reporter asked Trump a question he preferred to dodge, he referred it to Dr. Anthony Fauci, standing in a row of suits behind Trump. *Fauci.* I remembered him. During the AIDS crisis, Dr. Fauci was vilified by just about everyone. In the early 1980s, his colleagues questioned why he would waste his talents on a disease confined to "a handful of gay men." In 1981, the *New England Journal of Medicine* rejected his submission about potential spread as "alarmist." In 1989, Fauci met with members of ACT-UP, a tireless group of activists whose determination could not be denied, ultimately leading him to endorse the parallel-track program that made experimental treatments available to the terminally ill. Now, in 2020, Dr. Fauci was front and center again, calmly explaining what was known, but mostly unknown, about COVID-19—that is, when he was given a chance to speak.

The next morning, relief washed over me when I received my COVID test results. Turned out, my virus was just garden-variety flu. Still, with the threat of COVID looming, like everyone I knew, I retreated into an extreme social distancing routine, working remotely, zooming meetings. Facetime calls replaced hugs with my grandchildren, leaving me only to reimagine the feel of their tiny arms stretched around my neck, the beat of their precious hearts against mine. The emptiness of my arms made them ache.

Loneliness has a way of reordering one's priorities. At first, I busied myself with all those tasks I had been putting off: I cleaned and Marie-Kondoed my closet. I reorganized the den and bought an arc trainer, moving my workouts from the local gym to the basement. I turned my dining table into a mini-assembly line, cutting reams of donated fabric, then stitching and sending hundreds of handmade masks to the local hospital, then to friends. I retrieved batches of paperbacks from oversized Amazon boxes: new memoirs—*Educated, My Salinger Year, The Lie,* and the exquisite *Dear Mr. You.* I immersed myself in AIDS literature of various genres—*And the Band Played On, Borrowed Time, When We Rise,* and *Close to the Knives* among them.

When I wasn't reading, the TV—my constant companion— flashed images of the sick and dying. Nurses clad in trash bags begged for masks and personal protective supplies, and doctors pleaded for ventilators. Refrigerator trucks lined up outside Brooklyn Hospital Center to handle the overflow of corpses. Relatives of the sick and dying held homemade "I love you signs" outside hospital windows of quarantine wards. My heart ached at their pain and the memories these images triggered—of young men denied entry to a partner's bedside because they were not "family." Nearer to home, when my friends and acquaintances started to die of COVID, a different kind of lingering malaise set in, the result of sustained isolation and apprehension that no amount of busywork could alleviate. One truth had become glaringly apparent: none of us knew who would be next. And while we waited for news of a vaccine, I was skeptical.

By then, it was impossible to miss the myriad similarities between the COVID and AIDS pandemics. In both cases, the emergence of the disease was met with stunningly insufficient preparations and outright governmental denial. One of

President Reagan's first acts in 1981 was to cut the CDC budget by half, just before the first known cases of HIV-AIDS began to emerge. In an eerie echo of that pre-pandemic error, President Trump discarded the Obama administration's pandemic playbook and disbanded the NSC Council Directorate for Global Health Security and Biodefense, a decision which crippled the government's COVID response. Then, before the shutdown, Trump famously remarked of COVID, "One day—it's like a miracle—it will disappear." Similarly, in the early years of AIDS, President Reagan had steadfastly ignored the disease, never uttering the term "AIDS" until 1985. By then, 5,000 people had died.

Worse still, throughout 2020, as the numbers of dead and dying from COVID mounted, President Trump himself endorsed quack remedies, suggesting patients ingest the untested drug hydroxychloroquine, inject themselves with disinfectant and expose themselves to ultraviolet rays of light. During the AIDS crisis, scammers preyed on patients desperate for actual therapies, hawking everything from herbal remedies, lotions and potions to apply to the skin, chemicals like Virodene (derived from an industrial solvent), oxygen therapy and electronic zappers.

As if these indignities were not enough, scapegoating became as rampant during the era of COVID as it was during the AIDS pandemic. During Coronavirus Task Force briefings on television, President Trump's words set off a fire in my brain, especially his references to the "China Virus" and "Wuhan Flu." The xenophobia aside, what pierced my heart was the victim-blaming, as if the first to contract the virus were responsible for collectively incubating a deadly virus and then spreading it globally. I couldn't help recalling how HIV-AIDS, had once been called the "gay plague," "gay cancer," and "Gay-

Related Immune Deficiency" or "GRID." The implication: it happens to *them*. They brought it on themselves.

By the end of 2020, over six million Americans had been infected with COVID. With so many lessons of the eighties unheeded by the politicians and policymakers of 2020, the country was in freefall as we headed for the polls to vote in the national election. And as 2020 came to a close and our democracy teetered on the brink, so did our collective mental health. Illness had become our ethos. Confinement had turned us inward. Motion, activity, interaction, communion—all were lost to the nether world of technology-induced connections that felt artificial and forced. We retreated into ourselves; we pondered the time stolen from us—so many places we may have traveled, people we may have met, opportunities we may have missed.

For the next year, flashes of hope came in the form of vaccines and boosters—hopes that flickered as the virus mutated, assuming more infectious, vaccine-resistant forms. Online sources and local newspapers posted case percentages by county, breaking down the number of COVID deaths by vaccination status, by age, by gender, diminishing the human loss to data points. And just as in the last pandemic, our collective mood fluctuated from optimism to despair, depending on the latest surge, the release of a new booster, or news of a friend's premature death.

As the pandemic raged on, our COVID fatigue worsened. We missed the lives we'd had. We grieved for what we had lost: people, certainly, but also so many momentous events—graduations, weddings, reunions. We wanted our kids to play sports, act in school plays, go to dances; we wanted to go to parties and baseball games and concerts. We wanted our meetings across tables rather than cyberspace. We yearned not only to look into one another's eyes, but to see the whole of each and every precious face. We wanted to smother some of those faces with kisses.

We have reached a point when COVID no longer consumes our thoughts and actions. We hope that the worst is behind us. And while it is preferable to cast aside our COVID memories, choosing instead to rejoice in our ability to interact freely with one another once again, we should not forget. Complacency led us from HIV-AIDS to COVID. We must emerge more aware than ever that a pandemic can sneak up on us, invade our lives, take us down. We cannot know for certain whether or when another viral agent will materialize and if, this time, we will have learned from our mistakes, less likely to deny, obfuscate, and blame. All we can do is hope that we will be better prepared to meet the challenges ahead.

Yet, it is not merely the re-emergence of widespread illness that concerns me. A different kind of disease is endemic in the dark corners of our society: the disease of prejudice. Following a group of misguided politicians so determined to draw our attention from their own impotence, an entire segment of the population seems bent on proclaiming gayness a sickness rather than what it is: an innate aspect of one's God-given nature. Across the country, anti-LGBTQ bills are proliferating, fueling bias and threatening the gains that activists have worked so hard to bring to fruition. In Florida and Tennessee, legislation to regulate school curricula has essentially removed LGBTQ-themed literature and language from the discourse. In Iowa, Indiana, Louisiana, and Kentucky, limits or outright bans to access for gender-affirming care have become the norm. Anti-LGBTQ legislation has become so pervasive that Canada has issued a travel advisory to its LGBTQ citizens, encouraging them to research the laws in the state they plan to visit before traveling to the. United States. When other countries suggest that ours is hostile to a particular community, we do not do much to affirm the United States as a bastion of freedom.

I recognize in these trends the familiar agenda behind the ultra-conservative furor to drive us backward in time, to remake our culture to resemble the parochial climate of the 1950s and '60s in which Olaf and I grew up. In the midst of this fear-mongering, I hear the echoes of my brother's anguished voice saying, "They hate us, Holine." And I'm left to wonder how hating the other could have become a source of comfort to anyone.

Yet, resurging memories of a disheartened Olaf are transitory, inevitably overcome by the sheer force of his spirit. Instead, the Olaf I hear in my head is singing, joking in Italian, encouraging and uplifting me and others around him, his beloved piano tinkling in the background. And I am buoyed in the knowledge that his jubilance and positivity are hardly gone from the world, despite our trauma and strife.

Like Olaf, the optimists among us could not despair for long, even in the early stages of the COVID pandemic. Forging their own paths, many believed they could turn crisis into opportunity. Using the time in quarantine for reflection and redirection, they pursued productive goals, searching for something—anything—that could alter the trajectory of their lives. Some reimagined who they could be, reframing their futures and pursuing long withheld dreams. They quit jobs. They grew their hair out gray. They lost weight. They started businesses. They ended toxic relationships. They moved across the country, from the cold into warmth, from the darkness into light. With hope in their hearts, they transformed a tragic circumstance into a chance to live differently.

For my part, I did not move across the country, quit a job, or start a new business. I did not lose weight or end a relationship. I did not even let my hair go gray. I did, however, pursue a lifelong dream: I wrote. And in writing, I breathed my brother back to life with every keystroke, rediscovering his unique and precious essence.

It wasn't until I typed that last word of the last chapter that I realized: it wasn't I who had brought Olaf back. He was there all along, waiting for me to return to him. Instead, it was he who had brought me back.

Olaf had saved me once again.

ACKNOWLEDGMENTS

I am a firm believer that the most difficult projects are often the most worthwhile. I also believe that no one accomplishes an important goal alone. When I sometimes felt that writing this book was an unreachable pipedream, the embrace of a loving and supportive community of family, friends, mentors and editors made all the difference.

To my dear friends — Marie Czarnecki, Dick Friedrich, Ellis Searles, Shannon Farrell, John Bullis, Dennis Dewey: You read all or parts of assorted drafts (at various stages, both comprehensible and not-so-comprehensible). Your generosity of spirit is outmatched only by your unbridled encouragement and enthusiasm. When I questioned my own audacity at believing I could write a book, you told me that I could. You gave me confidence when I most needed it. You not only found redundancies and grammatical issues, questionable word choices and misplaced punctuation, you helped me find my own voice. I am so thankful for you all.

To my cousin Matthew Ginsburg, my ardent cheerleader, my spirit brother: You gave me recommendations and contacts, you sent me books and tickets to literary events, you texted me night or day when I had questions and insecurities (or just wanted to chat about the Yankees or the E Street Band). No one has a tighter schedule nor more pressures and deadlines, yet somehow you always found time for me. More importantly, you believed in my book from the first page. Passionate and hopeful, you never lost faith that I'd find a publisher, even when I wasn't so sure. I appreciate your sweet guidance and love more than I can express.

To my son-in-law, Ryan Miller, for your beautiful song and your genius technical skills: without you, I not only would not have a happy ending to Olaf's story — or a website! — but I would not have that surge of joy I experience every time I watch you with my grandchildren. I am so blessed to call you family.

To my writing mentor, friend, and confidant, Elizabeth Cohen, without whom there would be no book: it is hard to express my boundless gratitude. You challenged me at every turn, pushing me to change narration into scenes and dialogue and action, turning what began as a sort of diary into a living, breathing experience. You coaxed and cajoled, urging me to seek my "inner poet," and — when I veered into bad habits — to step away and *read* some poetry. You taught me hard lessons, sometimes cutting whole chapters, showing me that even if a writer has fallen in love with a passage, that passage may belong in another book. And when your comment in the margin was "I love Olaf," I knew I'd found the sweet spot. You are an endless inspiration. My fondness for you knows no bounds.

To my faithful editor, Samme Chittum, guru of language and beacon of wisdom: we were kindred spirits from the outset. I marvel at all that you know, at the care and humility and respect that underlies each and every editorial comment and suggestion. You once told me I had the "fire in my belly" that a good reporter needs, that I was brave to share a story so personal. You told me I "brought Olaf back to life," the highest compliment you could give me. You never wavered in your belief that Olaf's was a life that should be honored, that his story was a tale that must be told, and without you, it would not have been.

Elizabeth and Samme, because of you, what began as a story became a song.

To my darling daughter, Sara: you were beside me every single day, experiencing my insecurities and missteps, rejoicing in my achievements and successes. When I published an article, you were the one who rejoiced the loudest, sharing it with anyone who might listen (and even those who might not). You are my North Star, my heart, my legacy, my joy. And you loved your Uncle Olaf unconditionally, just as he loved you. He would have been so very proud of the woman you've become.

Finally, to my husband, Paul: for your infinite patience and love, especially during the trying times, through Olaf's illness and all of the many losses and tribulations since, I am most thankful. You not only experienced his death in real time, you listened to me read and reread the passages that carried us both back in time, sometimes to unhappy places. You never once doubted me, never left me wallowing alone in the past. You negate my worst tendencies: my worry, my cynicism, my what-ifs, my perfectionism. You counter them all with ridiculous optimism, unwavering positivity, childish fun and limitless love. You are sun to my shade, my music in human form, my Christmas Eve on a gray March day. You are my all.

ABOUT THE AUTHOR

Jennifer Boulanger is an activist, educator, and freelance journalist. An originator of the Safe Space initiative for local LGBTQ community college students, she holds a Master of Science degree in literacy from SUNY Cortland and a doctorate in Adult Education from Teachers College at Columbia University. She is an advocate for a New York refugee resettlement community in her community and serves as Vice President of Whitney's Legacy, a foundation dedicated to supporting and empowering women. She is a mother and grandmother of six, and lives in Central NY with her husband, Paul.